Dancing Madly Backwards

Paul Marechal

DANCING MADLY BACKWARDS

A Journey into God

Foreword by Morton Kelsey

CROSSROAD · NEW YORK

1982
The Crossroad Publishing Company
575 Lexington Avenue, New York, NY 10022

Library of Congress Cataloging in Publication Data

Marechal, Paul.
Dancing madly backwards.

Includes bibliographical references.
1. Spiritual life.   I. Title.
BV4501.2.M339   248.4   81–17285
ISBN 0–8245–0408–9 (pbk.)   AACR2

Acknowledgments

Specified excerpt abridged from "The Cry Going out over Pastures" (p. 59) in *This Body Is Made of Camphor and Gopherwood* by Robert Bly. © 1977 by Robert Bly. Reprinted by permission of Robert Bly.

Excerpts from *The Kabir Book,* copyright © 1971, 1977. Reprinted by permission of Robert Bly.

Excerpts from *Lorca and Jimenez,* copyright © 1977 by Robert Bly. Reprinted by permission of Robert Bly.

Excerpts from *News of the Universe,* reprinted by permission of Sierra Club Books from *News of the Universe,* copyright 1980 by Robert Bly.

Specified excerpt from "Shack Poem" (p. 8) in *Sleepers Joining Hands* by Robert Bly. © 1971 by Robert Bly. Reprinted by permission of Harper & Row, Inc.

Specified excerpts from "Sunday Morning in Tomales Bay" (p. 45) and "A Windy Day at the Shack" (p. 68) in *The Morning Glory* by Robert Bly. Copyright © 1975 by Robert Bly.

Excerpt from *Talking All Morning* (Ann Arbor: The University of Michigan Press), copyright © 1980 by Robert Bly. Reprinted by permission of Robert Bly.

Specified excerpt from "To Live" (p. 25) in *This Tree Will Be Here for a Thousand Years* by Robert Bly. Copyright © 1979 by Robert Bly.

Excerpt from "Doppelgänger" in *The Avenue Bearing the Initial of Christ into the New World, Poems 1946–1964* by Galway Kinnell. Copyright 1953,

1954, © 1955, 1958, 1959, 1960, 1961, 1963, 1964, 1970, 1971, 1974 by Galway Kinnell. Reprinted by permission of Houghton Mifflin Company.

W. S. Merwin, *The Lice.* Copyright © 1967 by W. S. Merwin. Reprinted with the permission of Atheneum Publishers.

W. S. Merwin, *The Moving Target.* Copyright © 1973 by W. S. Merwin. Reprinted with the permission of Atheneum Publishers.

Excerpts reprinted from *Mystical Poems of Rumi* by Jalal al-Din Rumi, translated by A. J. Arberry by permission of The University of Chicago Press. Copyright © 1968.

Excerpts from *Dismantling the Silence,* copyright © 1971 by Charles Simic. Reprinted by permission of the publisher, George Braziller, Inc.

Gitanjali by Rabindranath Tagore (New York: Macmillan, 1913). Excerpt reprinted by permission of Macmillan Publishing Co., Inc.

Excerpt from *The Branch Will Not Break.* Copyright © 1961 by James Wright. Reprinted by permission of Wesleyan University Press.

For My Parents, With Love

In sooth, Princess. I am an artist
of purest blood. A poet without poems,
a painter without paintings, a musician
without music, even an actor without a role.
The completed work . . . is dedicated
to . . . you. . . .

Ingmar Bergman

Contents

Foreword

The world is very mysterious. It is full of paradoxes and unfinished stories. Many of us try to avoid these paradoxes and finish the stories. Only a few step deliberately into this mystery, into the religious way.

Paul Marechal has been on this journey for many years. He put aside "the sentinel of the ego—a man in his twenties wearing dark glasses, a student of Descartes" and traveled wherever the path might lead. And now he shares that journey with those who are interested in this exciting venture.

The author records his journey in stories and narratives, in parables and images, in poetry and song. He tells us of those centers of meaning where transformation and new insights have come to him. He writes of the bleak wilderness and of silence, of city streets and of prophets, of ancient masters and their secrets, of the irreducible power of matter and the invincible quality of spirit, of death and love. These themes merge into one another and yet they are quite distinct. Throughout he traces the presence of the Secret Friend, a loving Friend we can encounter in all of these experiences.

The story of this journey will strike an authentic note in all who have traveled on the inner way and found themselves dancing madly backwards into the heart of reality.

But this little book is more. It is a call to spiritual adventure. Many of us cannot go upon such a trip without a guide. The author provides a picture map of places one may visit on that journey and hints and suggestions for what is required of our souls if we would go forth upon it.

First of all we are told of the silence in which every inner journey begins and to which it must return again and again. That silence is both a great joy and at times a great burden.

He speaks of the secret or hidden monk within each of us who longs for this inner journey. The outer monk is the living symbol for a reality in all of us, and this is why the monk exercises such a pull on the human imagination. Reading these reflections can feed this solitary one within.

Most of all this book sings of love, its inevitable presence and its undying power. Those who would find this love and hold it to them, must allow that love to be their inner motivation and guide. Our human love is stirred up by Divine Love and this human response leads us deeper and deeper into Love's mystery.

Some people may find that this story will actually take them on the journey itself. One finds in these reflections the continuity of a string of pearls. The reader will want to return many times both to the golden string upon which they are strung as well as to the individual jewellike stories and images.

In another way this book is more like a work of music which introduces theme after theme, builds upon them, varies them and brings them to an organic whole in a grand finale.

One could find many other images to express the story that Paul Marechal is telling. There are a limitless number of ways of speaking of both the goal of seeking and of the journey itself. The mystery at the center of God is delicately and powerfully revealed in this rare exposition of the journey into the other side of silence.

Morton Kelsey

A Bow of Gratitude

So many have helped to bring the gift of this book to others—and ultimately back to the Original Gift. Of these many, I would like to offer a bow of gratitude to the following: Richard Payne, Caroline Whiting, Dr. and Mrs. Robert Buffum, Charlene Moreau, Diane Frank, and Malane Collins. It was kind of Morton Kelsey to take time from his heavy schedule to write the foreword to this book.

I also want to thank Brother Casimir of Spencer for sharing his impressions of Iceland as we sat under the pine trees at Conyers one fall morning and watched Flannery O'Connor's peacocks.

Robert Bly says that two hours of solitude are about right for each line of poetry. This is not a book of poetry, but—with a few exceptions—every book needs a measure of solitude to flow into being. So another bow of gratitude is due—this time to those who by their hospitality offered me the gift of solitude: Charlie and Alyce O'Brien, the monks of Conyers, the sisters of Wrentham and the brothers at the chaplain's house, the monks of Oxford, the Oblates of Washington, D.C., Hollis and Terry Taggart, and the staff at Maryhill Retreat House—Fr. Bruce Miller, Sr. Elise Bengfort, and the Rev. Mr. Charles Jones.

Finally, my gratitude goes to the variety store—someplace in New England, I forget where—which inspired the title of this book. The new owners have decided to drop the original name. So now all that remains of "Dancing Madly Backwards" is the title of this book and the deep song that goes on day and night inside the heart of every pilgrim, as he flows with the rhythm of a Great Round Dance.

Note

The glossary at the end of the book provides the reader with a guide to pronouncing the non-English names and words found throughout the text.

Dancing Madly Backwards

Prologue

Far out at the edge of the heron's wing,
where the air is disturbed by the last feather,
there is the Kingdom. . . .
Robert Bly

Calcutta. A beggar, half-conscious, is lying on a mat in a home for the dying. A nun is kneeling by his side, her thin, angular face looking down at the man, her delicate fingers wiping his forehead with a washcloth. She is an Albanian peasant who went to India fifty years ago and never left, a Christ whose eyes shine like the wings of a heron flying around the sun, a silence whose light soars through the darkness, like the love songs of gypsies in Granada.

How can I describe the beggar's eyes as he summons all his strength to motion to the nun to draw closer?

She obeys.

It takes the beggar a long time to whisper something in her ears: "I have lived . . . like an animal . . . Now I will die . . . like an angel."

The beggar's final words.

* * *

A month later, near a tiny village north of Calcutta. The Albanian nun is smiling, half running toward a child she has not seen for a long time.

Now she is standing in front of him with folded hands. The boy is looking up at her, his head tilted to the left, just slightly. He is so thin, his pants way too big.

The child is a leper.

"*Namasté,*" the nun says.

"*Namasté,*" the boy answers, his hands folded, the voice coming from a place inside him far away. The voice of a Silent Seer, a Lover inside the child who knocks on doors with the hem of his rag-garment; a Pilgrim who fills the streets with his secret.

> Life is a secret; death is the key that opens it;
> but he who turns the key disappears forever into the
> secret.

The words of Maeterlinck in *Before the Great Silence.*

Wrong, the young leper thinks. Maeterlinck is right—yet wrong. Life is the key that opens the secret of life. Death is another, a deeper form of the turning key. The destiny of both life and death is to disappear into the secret, forever.

The secret of *Namasté.*

* * *

A January morning in New Delhi. The time: 1948.

Mahatma Gandhi asks his granddaughter, Ava, to bring him all the important papers. He has to respond right away: tomorrow may never come. . . .

Later that day, he is assassinated.

As he falls slowly to the ground, Gandhi brings his hands together in the traditional Indian custom: a final gesture of peace and forgiveness.

"*Namasté.*"

A key turns, a great light disappears, silence and love fall deeper into the secret of life and death.

The hands of India, and of the universe, come slowly together: without anger, without bitterness.

Only: *"Namasté."*

* * *

"Namasté."

This is how—with folded hands—Indians often greet each other, and how they part company.

Namasté paraphrases the Indian poet Kabir:

> . . . as the river gives itself into the ocean,
> what is inside me moves inside you.[1]

Namasté means: I revere the spaciousness inside you, the home of every living thing: the old man whispering psalms before an open window in the middle of the night, the Assyrian hound howling in one of Lorca's poems, the silence of the stars and all the seven oceans.

Namasté means: I esteem the love energy inside you, without which the moon would be a dusty hollow and the sun would never wake.

Namasté means: "I honor the place in you of love, of light, of truth, of peace. I honor the place within you where if you are in that place in you and I am in that place in me, there is only one of us."[2]

> I remember at daybreak,
> The air on the point of cooling
> Was just starting to heat up,
>
> I heard a voice in the distance,
> I looked up, far away,
> There at the beginning of the world
>
> I could make out a beggar,
> Down the long street he was calling *Galway!*
> I started towards him and began calling *Galway!* [3]

To the reader, *namasté.*

* * *

The heron in Robert Bly's poem—who is he?

Without the Great Blue Heron I would wander around, hands in my pockets, like a man waiting for a ride. But with him I wander—with a purpose. By the grace of the Great Blue Heron my silence flows into yours, I fold my hands in your presence, bright wings inside me whisper, *"namasté,"* again and again.

This Heron gives himself with gentle intensity, like a man who will never see his wife again, or Christ at the Last Supper. His love springs from a secret inside me—the world's secret—and rises up like a fount of water, day and night; even when the Heron seems to walk away ". . . like some old Hittite empire, all the brutality forgotten, only the rare vases left, and the elegant necks of the women . . ."[4]

This morning the Heron comes to me with news of an African storyteller who prefaces each tale by admitting, "This is a lie."

His audience knows what he means. The surface details and images of the tale—its shell—while not necessarily factual, express truth. The kernel of the tale is what counts, its point.

Not all that follows in these pages happened—in the historical sense. And yet Moshe, for one, did exist: at the level of symbol, which is as real as this body and these senses. So the informal notes that comprise this book are both kernel and shell, "truth" and "lie"—by the grace of the Great Blue Heron, whose bright wings have carried us into a kingdom of silence and of love, the kingdom on earth, as it is in heaven.

> And the heron slowly ascends, each wing
> as long as Holland . . .[5]

Blessed be the Great Blue Heron. He has made us in his image: gypsy castanets dancing madly backwards, singing deep melodies on wings as long as Holland; soaring with the beggar and the leper, and the nun with shining eyes, to an ecstasy of silence and of song.

My Home Is A Wilderness

This is a tale with a kernel.
You'll have to use your own teeth to crack it.
Charles Simic

My home is a wilderness of glaciers and geysers, a tale with a kernel, a wasteland where my companions are rugged coasts and canyons . . . and rocks. Thousands and thousands of rocks.

Christ stopped at Eboli, an Italian film says. But he did not stop here. Christ kept going, moving deeper into the haunting solitude of this wasteland with its shining rocks, and a wind which sways over the waters night and day. He was in his element here: inside the heart of a silent love which rings hope over the pale and lonely trees of this world, brooding in their heavy bodies.

Christ is still in this wasteland, where an old pianist and his wife walk arm in arm each day at dusk beneath the wind, sharing the language of ancient Norsemen. . . .

Christ did not stop here. He did not stop at this story with a kernel, where sea birds glide in and out of their homes in the cliffs, often the only sound you hear for hours, sometimes even days. But Christ stopped at Eboli. . . .

* * *

"Oddly domestic, strangely tended to"—the impression of an American visitor en route to Scandanavia.

He is right. Despite its wildness, this country looks oddly domestic, strangely tended to. Like the first day of creation, when the Holy One leaned over his child, his mercy shining like the wings of the Great Blue Heron.

This afternoon I come across a huge eider duck sitting in her nest, staring at me, with her body of fine soft down. I wonder what would happen if I went over there. . . .

When I reach the nest I extend my hand—slowly—to touch her beak. The duck does not draw back. Instead, she closes her eyes: a delicate symbol of the silence that connects her with me, and the friendship she offers—and receives—in this wasteland where everything is a friend who whispers: *"namasté."*

It could not be otherwise. This is not Eboli. It is the place Christ loves, his home: the unaccountable fragrance of the rocks, the wind glittering in the darkness.

* * *

And the silence of *yom ehad.*

Last night, after praying Compline in the darkness, the final verse of the last psalm began to move around inside me, like the Spanish *canto hondo*—deep song. I found myself cooperating with this music, leaning into it, knowing that when its last note vanished into the silence, another leaf would be living on the tree I call "myself."

"The maker of heaven and earth," the last psalm ends—the maker of *yom ehad,* a time when everything was in God's womb—and yet out of the womb. A time when whatever was, was—and yet flowed in the heart of God.

Yom ehad: day one.

This is what the Hebrew Bible calls the first stirring of creation. It speaks of a formless wilderness, of darkness, of light. The only sign of life is *ruah:* a wind, a divine presence soaring over the waters. And nothing else.

The wings of *ruah* are still swaying over the waters of this wilderness I call home. *Yom ehad* is still here, in this desert of rocks, Christ's sanctuary, where the first lines of the Book of Genesis are being written—and rewritten—every day.

Tonight the rays of the full moon are gleaming over the purple and rust of the rocks. Normally we see just one side of the moon. But tonight its barren spaces have rotated so that both edges are peeking down at me. The heavens are confirming the secret of every wilderness, and its two sides.

I am body, mind, senses, imagination, feelings: one side. But I am also a man who lives way down inside the kernel of a "tree": the other side.

* * *

Everything in creation is a kernel inside a tale: a quince blossom opening up, revealing its unspoken language, an energy that moves softly, like the Christ who stopped at Eboli.

Vaster than the spheres, older than the canyons of the west and the mountains of the east, it is the luminous body of blind trees and deep hollows; and of the love humming through the wind on a solitary night in the wilderness, when after years of transformation an old man changes into a child—in the Gospel sense.

* * *

Somewhere in the world tonight, in places where monks still rise from their sleep in the darkness of the night to sing psalms to a Secret Friend, a fire will be lit and a candle blessed; and a monk will take up the Bible and read the opening lines from the Book of Genesis: "On day one God made the heavens and the earth, a wilderness without form. . . ."

Tonight, in the darkness of the Paschal Vigil, someone in this tiny village will light a fire and bless a candle, and take up the same text, and whisper its silence into the wilderness: "On day one. . . ."

* * *

Christ stopped at Eboli. But he stayed here.

Curious, I think, after the Vigil has ended: you would think that with every passing second this place would be closer to day two.

It isn't.

Not here, not in this wasteland. Nor will it happen tomorrow, or the day after, or ever.

Here it will always be day one.

The Rocks

He clave the rocks in the wilderness,
and gave them drink as out of the great depths.
Psalm 78

"I feel as though I'm being watched."

"What did you say?" Gunnar said, looking up quickly.

"I don't know what it is. Maybe the position of the sun, or the lack of vegetation. But wherever I go, I feel as though something—or someone—is watching me."

The Icelander leaned forward and studied his American guest intently.

"I'm amazed to hear you say that. Amazed, not because you notice this, but because you've noticed it so *quickly*. It means you are a true Icelander. You're experiencing what everyone here grows up with, and senses—sooner or later."

"Which is . . . ?"

"The feeling of being watched."

The American leaned forward and plunged his gaze into the Icelander.

"Watched by whom? By what?"

"By the rocks. The rocks are watching."

"The *rocks?*"

"Remember what I told you about my geology research in the wilderness for a month? That's when I first felt I was being watched. It was a physical experience, actually very comforting—like a delicate presence tending to me. But frankly, I was glad to get back to town, and the sound of people moving, their voices, their laughter. . . ."

The American's eyes rounded.

"Gunnar—you're saying the *rocks* are watching us?"

"More than the rocks, my friend. Much more. You may know that Tolkien did the research for his trilogy here. Icelanders believe that the first inhabitants of this country are watching. The hobbits are looking out of the rocks. . . ."

"Gunnar, be serious!"

"Hobbits, or whatever you choose to call them. Let's say hobbitlike creatures: friendly, small. And mischievous—they love to play tricks on people. It's not unusual for them to break into houses and run off with food. Some say they eat as much as six times a day. I don't know, I haven't seen them, only felt them all around, watching. . . ."

* * *

Hobbits? Just hobbits? Or is the Icelander explaining a deeper experience in terms familiar to his culture?

Hobbits? Or is the Icelander conscious of a vaster, a deeper presence, of which the rocks and hobbits are symbols?

Could it be that the Icelander is sensing the basic element of life: an intense, loving awareness pervading every pocket of creation? A spaciousness without father or mother, a kernel singing quietly, no notes missing?

When—in another time, another culture—the psalmist felt this same song watching him, he took up his harp and sang back:

> Whether I stand or sit,
> whether I walk or lie down,
> You are watching me, Yahweh.
>
> Whether I ascend to the heavens,

or descend to the depths of Sheol,
Your Hand is always with me, Yahweh.

Christ stopped at Eboli. But he stayed here.

* * *

In every place and every era, this Secret Friend watches the same script unfold, again and again.

Luminous words pass from the high consciousness of the master to the lower awareness of the disciple. The pupil transmits the teaching to his own disciples at their level. And the scenario goes on.

Far from Iceland, in another era, a Jewish master is speaking with one of his disciples. The young man is impulsive, intense, full of ideals—and immature.

"I will build my people on this rock."

This confuses the pupil. The teacher has changed his name to Kefa—rock—to identify the disciple as the image of the Holy One, and now he is going to build his people on this rock?

"I don't understand."

Kefa's attention winds slowly around the master, like a schoolboy looking out at the rain.

* * *

In biblical times, to change a person's name—as from Abram to Abraham, or Saul to Paul—marks the beginning of a decisive change. Energy has begun to shift from the sleeping man entangled in himself, out of touch with his inner freedom —to his depth, flowing from the heart of a Secret Friend.

In Kefa's case—as with Abraham and Paul—his "original features" are coming into focus, an identity praised by the psalmist in his song to the rocks: "Your knowledge overwhelms me, Yahweh. Your watching was with me at the beginning, when your hands knitted me together in my mother's womb, in the image of a Secret Friend."

The potential image of God—silence, love, light—has

begun to unfold into likeness: a slow and delicate process, a pilgrimage of awakening. A few steps at a time, once the sleeping man comes to his senses. . . .

* * *

"I will build my people on this rock."

"I don't understand."

And because his pupil does not understand, the teacher reaches into the future for a story: about Dov Ber—also known as the Maggid of Mezritch—and what happened one night when the Maggid met the great master of the Jewish tradition: the Baal Shem Tov, or Besht.

Dov Ber was an unusual man. People trembled when they saw him. He never laughed. Tenacious, the Maggid was set in his ways, a Talmudic scholar who believed fervently in self-inflicted pain. He was known to fast from one Sabbath to the next, several times in a row. But eventually Dov Ber's attachment to penance caught up with him. He fell seriously ill, and doctors could do nothing more. But as a last hope someone suggested, "Why not see the Baal Shem Tov?"

Even though the Maggid disapproved of the visionary's path—the Besht sought to alleviate suffering, while the Maggid was sure that life should be a struggle—he gave in.

It was midnight when the Baal Shem Tov, dressed in a coat of wolf fur turned inside out, handed the Maggid the Book of Splendor. Dov Ber read aloud for a page when the Besht suddenly interrupted.

"Something is missing," the Baal Shem Tov said. "Something is lacking in your knowledge."

"And what is that?"

"Soul."

From that point on, the room was a mass of Fire. A brilliant light extended from wall to wall—a radiance that had been present all along, secretly watching the Maggid read.

After two hours of this—two hours at the center of creation—the Maggid got up to leave.

"Wait," the Besht said. "I won't let you go without a blessing."

And Israel Baal Shem Tov, the Master of the Good Name, bent his head to receive a blessing.

* * *

The sequel: years later, seven Hasidic masters are seated around a table in the House of Study. The Maggid of Mezritch, now a successor of the Baal Shem Tov, is praying the Scriptures. Suddenly a door opens and the Maggid appears, radiant with the light of Sinai, like Christ transfigured before Peter, James, and John on Mount Tabor. Terrified, five of the teachers run into the streets. A sixth hides under a table. Only Rebbe Wolfe stands his ground, applauding the scene with gusto.

* * *

And is Kefa, like the Maggid, the successor of his teacher?

The story of Dov Ber had no impact on him. He understood its meaning even less than he grasped his teacher's words, "I will build my people on this rock."

Why didn't he understand?

Because the time was not ripe. He had to wait, and follow the Maggid's pattern. All the ingredients of Dov Ber's story were present when a wind began to stir on the morning of Pentecost: light, humility, strength, silence, miles and miles of love.

This luminous wind filled the room of the disciples on Pentecost. The wind of *yom ehad,* leading Kefa as it did Abraham leaving for the wilderness: an old man without maps or compass, starting a journey into the land of likeness.

* * *

Like the Maggid, Kefa's story has a sequel.

Years later, the Seer of the Great Blue Heron, an old man with bright eyes, who has changed into what St. Peter calls "the hidden man of the heart," sits barefoot at his desk writing a letter to his friends: "You've tasted how good the Secret One is. So have I. . . ."

> He is the living rock. And you, my friends, are consecrated to sing the praises of this Secret Friend, who has led you into his marvelous light. Once you were no people; now you are God's people. Once you knew no mercy; now you are all mercy—the silence and love of the Secret One, our rock, our refuge. . . .
> *(version of I Peter 2:3, 4, 9–10)*

The letter had soul.

* * *

I've come to love this Iceland. Christ walked here, after fleeing into the sea, when the moneychangers tried to crown him king of the marketplace.

This is where he confronted the stranger dressed in a costume of dragon scales gleaming in the dark. It was a good disguise, but Christ knew better.

"Just bread?" he said. "People live by more than bread. . . ."

Blessed be the rocks of this Iceland, and the kernel inside them. Blessed be the secret of the Secret One, whose waters flow inside these rocks. Blessed be the Holy One, who watches over the bent trees of this world, whose blind eyes are the silence of the rocks they hear.

The Rebbe

Something goes through the world
Without speaking to anyone.
When it falls in water
It doesn't splash, when it enters a tree
It doesn't rustle.

The less you hear it the fiercer its presence is.
Time stops . . .

Charles Simic

Each author uses words for a different reason.

Elie Wiesel, a survivor of Auschwitz, admits that his writing is a *matzeva:* an unseen tombstone in memory of the unburied dead. Others write because they must. Like Nikos Kazantzakis, who wanted to run to the street corners and beg passersby for a little of their time—a quarter of an hour, anything—only enough to let him finish his work.

Others write to make a living. And still others, to share an insight, or an experience.

But some writers have no insights, no experiences, only questions. They use words to understand themselves, people, creation, God. Each in a different sequence.

And the wilderness? Its only memory is the Mercy of a

secret garden, where hundreds and thousands of apples and pears arrive, even in winter.

Urgency to convey an insight, to create a work of art, to make a living? The wilderness grows from the Gift; it returns to the Gift, inside the silence of Wings long as Holland.

Questions? The wilderness has none. Its life is a paradox beyond questions, the secret of a sky which keeps expanding farther and farther. . . .

Listen.

Low voices in the canyon, where the wind sweeps over long trails, and waits for Christ to speak his word into the night.

"Something is burning in those trees."

Avila: Teresa doing flamenco. The waves of a river on fire, leaning into the shore of the sky, like Fray Juan de la Cruz.

The desert of Egypt, in the fourth century: a hermit weaver throwing his shuttle back and forth, back and forth. . . .

The silence of the rocks who speak, timeless.

Drop a rock into the water: you hear no sound. Send it into a tree: nothing. The rocks talk to no one: their silence speaks from inside, as from Fire to fire.

Christ talks to no one in the wilderness. He speaks with everyone, as from Vine to branches.

The branch with the Fire inside is not the Fire: "I am not the Gift," the weaver challenges.

"And the Gift," a flamenco voice adds. "*Also* the Gift."

The words come from a deep song of paradox, the music not of Avila or Granada, but of the rocks who watch in the wilderness.

When Christ speaks, the paradox goes up in flames.

* * *

Low voices, farther up along the trail. Dawn is near.

"I wouldn't go in there."

It is the hermit: hesitant, unconvinced. He still has questions.

The flamenco woman is patient. Fine, she says, work

through the questions. But in the meantime, rivers of light are pouring through the sand, and bells no one hears are ringing in the garden. . . .

"I still wouldn't go in there."

"Into the paradox? Friend, there is no escaping paradox, not if you've come this far. When the sentinel of the ego—a man in his twenties wearing dark glasses, a disciple of Descartes—goes off to read, things begin to happen. The Baal Shem Tov's room goes up in flames. Dov Ber becomes All Fire, terrifying the teachers. Christ is transfigured on Mount Tabor, uplifting Peter, James, and John. But to see this it's not enough to be a weaver—or even a hermit in the desert; you have to stand inside the Rock, and sing like Moshe."

* * *

It was a beautiful Swiss summer day when I first saw him: a man with ruddy cheeks, wearing a black hat and shell-rimmed glasses. His eyes were radiant.

He was more than an old man strolling through a dense crowd of tourists and window shoppers in Interlaken. He was more than the silence I sensed as he passed by the shop, his head erect, greeting the shopkeeper and me. He was more than the black I saw as he moved slowly into the distance, tipping his black hat to the old woman at the fruit stand; this old man in his black suit and tie.

I watched him until the farthest shadow of his silence had moved on, leaving not a trace of black to linger behind.

I turned to Helmut, the Swiss shopkeeper.

"Who was that—the man in black who passed us a minute ago?"

"Him? That's Moshe. Look. Let me show you."

He pulled out a piece of paper and wrote: *Rebbe.*

"Reh-bee," Helmut said, smiling, with a trace of indulgence in his voice. "See? A spiritual master—Jewish."

"You know him?"

"Well, he keeps to himself. That's for sure. Himself and his people. But—yes, I know him. Better than anyone in Interlaken, outside of his people. When he first came here I was confused. I had trouble sleeping, and my marriage was going from bad to worse. I questioned everything. I knew I had to talk with someone; I had been searching for something deeper, more essential—and finding nothing. It was like going through those Chinese boxes, one inside another, on and on, always coming up empty-handed. Do you understand?"

I nodded.

"When I met Moshe, I knew instinctively that he had been sent here by some Secret Hand—to listen to me. So I asked him if we could get together, and when we did. . . ."

His conversation with the Rebbe sounded remarkably like a dialogue from one of Elie Wiesel's books:

> "I'm searching."
> "What are you searching for?"
> I was going to correct him: "whom," not "what."
> But I got hold of myself and answered: "I don't
> know yet."
> He was not convinced.
> "What are you looking for?"
> I said: "For an answer."
> His voice was cutting: "An answer to what?"
> I was going to correct him: "to whom," not
> "to what." But I looked for the simplest way out:
> "To my questions. . . ."
> "Ah," he said, "you have questions, you?"
> "Yes, I do have some."
> He held out his hand.
> "Give them to me. . . ."[1]

"He sounds like an *abba*," I said. "A desert father."

"Abba?"

"Monk. The desert fathers were the first monks of Christendom. They lived in the fourth century, and left the cities and towns to go into the deserts of Egypt, Palestine, and Syria. The *abba* committed himself to a radical solitude, inner and outer, and by doing that opened himself to God's love. . . ."

The shopkeeper cut me off in mid-sentence. He sounded irritated.

"I don't know about all that," he said, as though to himself. "Moshe is also a pilgrim. He never stays anywhere for long: Paris, Strasbourg, Vienna, Mallorca, Madrid. . . . The longest he stayed in any one place was Auschwitz, where he had no choice."

"Auschwitz? The concentration camp?"

"Yes," Helmut said, fidgeting. "I tried to ask him about it but he changed the subject. Abruptly. He began to talk about the Rebbe who, once a year, would sit in the seclusion of his room and receive his disciples. You know how? By allowing the voices of his disciples to flow into his ears from the four ends of the earth. He insisted he wasn't talking about himself, that this was from the Hasidic tradition, but I tend to think he was."

I told the shopkeeper the old man's journey reminded me of some of the early Christian monks, for whom pilgrimage was a way of life: a response to a special call. . . .

Again Helmut cut me off.

"Something else."

"What did you say?"

"Something else. He's a pilgrim, not a seeker. Do you understand? Moshe goes from place to place, moving deeper into the sky—a sky we would see if we could see."

> The blue sky opens out farther and farther . . .
> a million suns come forward with light,
> when I sit firmly in that world.
>
> I hear bells ringing that no one has shaken,
> inside "love" there is more joy than we know of,

rain pours down, although the sky is clear of clouds,
there are whole rivers of light.
The universe is shot through in all parts by a single
sort of love. . . .[2]

"See?" the shopkeeper said. "He's not looking for the sky.
He's looking *into* the sky. Better: the sky is calling him deeper
into its heart. He's different, this Moshe. He doesn't hate the
Germans. Can you imagine that? After Auschwitz?"

* * *

That afternoon I saw him again: Moshe, telling one of Dov
Ber's stories to a young man paralyzed from the waist down,
sitting in a wheel chair.

According to the Maggid, whenever the Baal Shem Tov
would eat, an angel would sweep down from the sky and
transform the food into an offering of fire.

How marvelous is that garden, where apples and pears,
both for the sake of the two Marys,
are arriving even in winter.

Those apples grow from the Gift, and they sink back
into the Gift.

It must be that they are coming from the garden to the
garden.[3]

An offering from Gift to gift. And from friend to Friend.

A Different Kind of Rebbe

*It was the "Selishter Rebbe" who told me one day:
"Be careful with words, they're dangerous. Be wary of
them. They beget either demons or angels. It's up to
you to give life to one or the other. Be careful, I tell
you, nothing is as dangerous as giving free rein to
words."*

Elie Wiesel

Elie Wiesel ends one of his chapters with the Selishter Rebbe
standing over his shoulder. The Rebbe is looking, judging his
disciple as he tries to express himself: Is he enriching the world
with his words? Is he giving birth to angels by his deeds?

But in the silence of the wilderness one becomes aware of
a Rebbe who watches without judging; the radiant figure in
one of Gerard Manley Hopkins's poems:

> The Holy Ghost over the bent
> World broods with warm breast
> and with ah! bright
> wings.[1]

*   *   *

What happens when we die?

Dr. Raymond Moody has done extensive research with
subjects pronounced clinically dead, and later restored to life.

After death the subject finds himself in a "spiritual" body: weightless as the rays of the sun, unrestricted by age, timeless. Communication is through thought transference.

A common element in the accounts of these subjects is a rendezvous with a "being of light," who unseals memories and goes straight to the heart of the matter: "How much have you learned—and loved?"

An interesting question, when we recall that in the Gospels Christ makes "giving" the criterion for "life success." The same criterion accompanies the pilgrim as he carries his life history across an open checkpoint, and into his rendezvous with the Being of Light.

"Have you enriched the world with your words? Have you given birth to angels by your deeds?"

The subject feels accepted, secure, at ease with this luminous "Someone," who leaves a comforting impression: much the way the rocks affected the geologist in the wilderness. But the comparison weakens when you understand what these people are feeling as they sense the qualities of this Secret Friend: strength, warmth, indescribable love, perfect understanding.

As if words could convey the breakthrough to the journey's Origin, and its End. Or what happens when branches and leaves rejoin roots, and roots open into the silence of the rocks.

* * *

The Secret Friend supports the subject throughout the "review": a time when vivid images from his life history roll past his awareness in sequence, like the hands of a clock going round and round.

Some scenes are good, some not so good.

The Light sees it all, and his watching is pure: a love energy rushing at immense speed into the subject's subtle body, like the Heron soaring into the heavens.

The Light refuses to judge—and so does Christ, who watches out of the luminous rocks over the burning wilderness, and over Eboli,

> . . . with warm breast
> and with ah! bright
> wings.[2]

* * *

"Christ, Rebbe, Being of Light."
But there are other names for God.
In India, Kabir, a fifteenth-century poet, called God the "Secret One."[3]

Kabir's intense life flowed with continuous love energy: "as the river gives itself into the ocean, / what is inside me moves inside you."[4] Kabir was married and a father. He earned his living at home as a weaver, throwing his shuttle back and forth, waiting for patterns to emerge—and all the while he was a pilgrim. Like Moshe, Kabir belonged to a tradition of pilgrimage which travels in everyone's heart—a tradition where home is the silence of delicate robins in an open field, and the ruby of the human heart, and the shining body of the Secret One.

Another poet, Jalal al-Din Rumi, belonged to the same tradition. Rumi lived in Turkey in the thirteenth century—but Turkey was not his only home. His poems are ecstatic, describing how it feels to share life with the One he called the "Friend." Rumi is like the blue jay in one of James Wright's poems:

> In a pine tree,
> A few yards from my window sill,
> A brilliant blue jay is springing up and down, up and
>   down,
> On a branch.
> I laugh, as I see him abandon himself
> To entire delight, for he knows as well as I do
> That the branch will not break.[5]

Jesus was another pilgrim: a luminous being who roamed inside the lowlands of friends and the friendless, and in the back country of the washed and the unwashed. With no place to lay his head, everyone was his refuge, every place his home.

Peter recognized his teacher's pilgrimage: "Where are you going?"

"You can't follow me now. But you will later."

"Why not now? I'll lay down my life for you."

"The rooster will crow three times, and when he is done, you will have denied me three times. But it doesn't matter, Peter. I want you to be where I am, and where I will always be."

Christ is still a pilgrim, traveling inside a paradox Peter could not fathom: a man going to his destiny, yet already in the Heart of Destiny.

> Far in the west the black mountain stands
> Around which our racers run at noon.
> Who is this man running with me,
> The shadow of whose hands I see?[6]

"Destiny," Christ says quietly to Peter. "Destiny is running with me. And with you."

But Peter is not satisfied. He wants his teacher to be more precise.

> Who is this man running with me,
> The shadow of whose hands I see?[7]

Jesus whispers the name.

"Abba."

Christ chooses this rare and tender Aramaic title to designate the Secret One as "Father," in the sense of a Love Which engenders life.

Abba, our Secret Destiny.

* * *

"Macao?" Moshe said. "I remember it well. A Portuguese town near Canton. Chinese gunboats in the shallow harbor, casinos, soldiers peering out of sentry boxes on the marshes. And the smugglers—lots of them—and the impressive Barrier Gate that separates Macao from the mainland of China. But what I remember most is the flamboyant cathedral on the hilltop. I was struck by how distant it appeared, how aloof. I felt its only connection with Macao was to look down—with a curl of disdain—at the half-castes, and the statue of Vasco Da Gama . . . staring back with equal disdain."

Moshe paused for a moment.

"The sky has always fascinated the religious imagination of mankind. Have you heard of the legend of the mystical flight, and of the rites of ascent and climbing? We can trace all of these myths and legends to a celestial symbolism that depicts the transcendent: the above, the beyond. That cathedral on the hilltop should have symbolized the transcendent: a depth beyond our senses and thoughts, present everywhere. But it didn't. The transcendent is not distant, but very near—and very comforting. It rises up from the unseen roots of every living being. It nourishes, sustains. So why did the cathedral leave me with a different impression? Maybe it was the architecture: a façade of Jesuit baroque. . . ."

Moshe paused again.

"The cathedral was built on rock—yet seemed detached even from the rock. Incongruous. Meister Eckhart questioned how you could ever divide anything white from whiteness. . . ."

Moshe looked at me and smiled.

"Well, my friend, you understand that these are subjective impressions. You might go to Macao and find it different."

* * *

It was as Moshe had said: a cathedral, miles away on a hilltop, its fingers touching the heavens, staring down at

Macao with a look of disdain. The cathedral: its gaze sweeping past Macao, settling on a plaza miles away, where a million pilgrim hands rise slowly above their heads, following the energy of long rivers of light. . . .

In a cobblestoned alley of Macao, a street beggar, a half-caste, stops me. He says he has a message from someone, a voice calling from far away: "Go to the hilltop, and see for yourself."

I obey.

Halfway up the hill, I pause and look down on the masts of the junks in the harbor, and the ferryboat plying to Hong Kong, an hour away. Strange drums are rolling in the distance. I wonder what they could be. . . .

I continue my journey to the cathedral built on rock.

By the time I reach the hilltop, the sun has gone down. The vacant eyes of the casino miles below are staring up at me. No birds are singing here. No trees anywhere. Everything is pale, empty.

I am alone.

A mild wind is sweeping around the façade of the immense cathedral.

In ruins.

A fire, Moshe said. He didn't know how it happened.

All that remains is the façade of Jesuit baroque, alone in the silence, detached from the heavens, a stranger to Macao. White without whiteness, asleep, tangled up inside itself.

A psalm without a heart.

All that remains is the façade . . . and the rock which once upheld the cathedral, and now upholds the Barrier Gate, and the bodies and senses of the smugglers of Macao, and the silence of the hermit in his wilderness.

In the whiteness, the rock is not alone.

The Rebbe is there, and so is the Secret One—and the other names: Friend, Abba, God.

Many names, but only One Name, watching in the whiteness over Eboli: caring from the Silence where a million hands have sealed themselves in Rock, and endless rivers of Light, and a Vine that never breaks.

Abba, Namasté

Inside this clay jug there are canyons and
    pine mountains, and the maker of canyons
    and pine mountains!
All seven oceans are inside, and hundreds of
    millions of stars.
The acid that tests gold is there, and the one
    who judges jewels.
And the music from the strings no one touches,
    and the source of all water.

If you want the truth, I will tell you the truth:
Friend, listen: the God whom I love is inside.
                        Kabir

A door opens, a door closes. A friend leaves, and is seen no more.

Judaism is not known for its tradition of monasticism, and yet—to the very end, when the angel of death came knocking on his door—Moshe was a monk.

So are you.

Not in the sense of one who takes vows, lives in a monastery, wears a monastic robe—although in rare cases it could mean that. But in the sense of one who increasingly hurls himself into subtler layers of inner depth. A monasticism not of structure, but of "this clay jug": the heart, with its hundreds of millions of stars.

The Greek root of "monk" is *monos:* one. The word implies a oneness beyond division or multiplicity. It underscores the instinct to transcend boundaries, to pass over into the freedom of nonduality: "not two."

The monasticism of "this clay jug" leaps beyond religious and cultural borders. It never speaks of a Christian heart or a Jewish heart or a Buddhist heart—but only of the human heart of Jesus, of Moshe, of Buddha.

The passion of *monos* burns in every heart, if only in seed form, often unsuspected: as a tiny spark of fire. It desires to be the harmony of "this clay jug": one with canyons and pine mountains and people, and the maker of all the seven oceans. *Monos* was Christ's desire when he said, referring to each monk of every age: "Abba, this is what I want: that they may be one in us."

The wholeness of "this clay jug" is also the harmony of *yom ehad,* when everything was one with—yet other than—God. The oneness toward which this inner monasticism flows is the secret of the first lines of the Book of Genesis, rewritten each day in the wilderness, amid the silence of the rocks, and the delicate presence of *Ruah.*

Ruah is a Hebrew word meaning spirit, breath, wind. The secret of *monos* is also the secret of *Ruah,* the mysterious "wind" which sweeps over the wilderness day and night. Being both male and female, the gender of *Ruah* suggests the value of wholeness. It implies the blending of the "maleness" and "femaleness" of the Secret One: activity and rest, creative power and gentle silence, the strength of fidelity and tender kindness.

The passion of inner monasticism resembles the desire of the Spanish poet Federico Lorca, which Robert Bly describes as "flying, hurtling through the air, like a tornado, putting new leaves on every tree it touches, writing as if he belonged to Cretan civilization—on whose murals there are no brutal kings, only bluebirds and winged griffins—a desire for intensity as immense as Dickens's characters' desire for food, a psyche so alive it doesn't like or dislike walls but flies over them."[1]

This drive, surging through the heart of every human tree, involves a paradox of unity and diversity; a silent devotion which, like Lorca's desire, puts new leaves on every tree it touches.

Devotion floats up from the silence of nonduality, where the devotee and his beloved are one. And yet devotion implies relationship, which in turn implies difference: otherness. But not at the expense of unity.

> The ship, solid and black,
> enters the clear blackness
> of the great harbor . . .
>
> Quiet. Silence.
> Silence which in breaking up at dawn
> will speak differently.[2]

Silence: an energy which extends beyond the furthest reaches of the universe—and never vanishes, a quiet which pervades every particle of this world, and glides through the blackness of the great harbor by night, and speaks differently by day.

Speech is the body of silence, like the word *namasté,* whispering the secret of "this clay jug." The word floats up from silence; it flows back into silence. The word of relationship and the quiet of the heart are inseparable—like love and the silence from which it is born, and the rest to which it returns, unceasingly.

Namasté is Christ's silent devotion to Abba. It is a word he shares with his beloved: the canyons, the mountains, the old man whispering psalms before an open window. . . .

Abba, *namasté.*

* * *

Silent devotion implies a triple paradox: the monk is one with—and yet other than—God, others, creation.

The first component of this paradox is "the festival of innocence": a gift of the Secret One. To live this festival is to share the life and innocence of God, and to see and to touch with the eyes and fingers of a Secret Friend. The devotee breathes a tranquillity that is divine: the silence of the Gift who carries his gift from garden to garden, unfolding new leaves, untangling roots, opening psalms in the sky.

But this life is also festive, dynamic, full of ecstatic love— soaring high in the air, with the joy of the archer in Nikos Kazantzakis's *Odyssey:* "as though he'd shot his soul into the sun. . . ."[3]

Which is a good description of Teresa of Avila, "that supremely 'flamenco' woman."[4] Teresa's "flamenco" is a dance of unity and diversity, a blend of nonduality and relationship. On the one hand the soles of her feet touch no ground, her limbs move without moving, her ears hear no melody. Teresa is lost in the Secret One—beyond thoughts, images, the distinction between "I" and "You."

And yet Teresa's dance is as vigorous as the archer shooting his soul into the sun, or a gypsy in love, doing flamenco before a campfire in the heart of Andalusia. Teresa's flamenco love flows out to her brothers and sisters with intensity, and with equal passion to the Risen Christ.

Still lost in the silence of the Secret One, Teresa dances with the Friend who is Other—physically present, yet in different form: a Luminous Being whose fragrance touches the farthest reaches of the universe and "this clay jug." The Christ who passed through doors after the Resurrection, like the light that swept through the room of the Baal Shem Tov.

* * *

As the monk moves deeper into the festive innocence of the Secret One, the paradox expands. The arms of silent devotion widen to embrace people, and every facet of the universe—the way Teresa did, and Moshe:

> His touch is gentle.
> It weighs a tear.
> It takes the mote out of the eye.[5]

To have a "compassionate heart" means to burn with love for every pocket of creation—because the box-elder is not other, the canyon not opposite, the pine mountain not an object of conquest. And yet it also means to have a flamenco heart that rejoices in diversity: a silence which whispers "*namasté*" to the sacred presence of the pine mountain, and the unique fragrance of the box-elder and the canyon.

Could this be the deepest meaning behind that gesture in *The Brothers Karamazov*—when the old monk Zossima, awaiting the angel of death, advises his young disciple Alyosha to reenter the "world" to serve the Secret One and his people?

Zossima leaves his body, and the young man—filled with the passion of *monos*—hurls himself to the earth in a gesture of silent devotion.

Ani Ledodi

Love giving itself, losing itself and finding itself in love,
and Love returning to itself, giving itself back in love—
this is the eternal pattern of the universe. . . . The nucleus
throws out its protons and electrons and they circle
round it, held by the attraction of Love. The sun throws
out its planets and they circle round it, held by the same
attraction. . . . Beyond the molecules and atoms, beyond
the protons and electrons, . . . there is an energy, a force
of life, . . . continually welling up from the abyss of being
in the Father, continually springing up into the light of
the Word, continually flowing back to its source in the
bliss of love. . . .

Bede Griffiths

"The eternal pattern of the universe." This, in the end, is what
Rebbe Zvi-Hersh of Ziditchoiv must have wanted to hear
when he hid in Rebbe Barukh's study one day.

Later on he told his friends what he had seen: an ecstatic
master, All Aflame, like the Maggid of Mezritch in the House
of Studies. But there was more: he had heard Rebbe Barukh
pray a verse from the Song of Songs—a set of love poems from
the Old Testament—with such passion that even he, Rebbe
Zvi-Hersh, had flown into ecstasy.

The verse?
Ani ledodi.

Meaning: "My Beloved, the Secret One, belongs to me—
and I belong to Him."[1]

Ani ledodi: the love-secret of the Hasid Barukh, and of
Moshe, and of each monk of every age and every culture.

* * *

Hasid and its plural, *Hasidim,* are terms derived from another Hebrew word, *hesed,* loving-kindness, which means that
every monk is a *Hasid:* not in the sense of belonging to the
movement founded by the Besht in the eighteenth century—
although it could mean that, but in the more sweeping way the
psalms describe the term: one who loves, and is first loved by,
the Secret One.

Slowly, gradually, the *Hasid* matures into the tree of the
opening lines of the psalter: a radiant body living near running
water, prospering in all it does, with leaves which never with-
er: "I can do everything in the Secret One who gives me
strength—the strength of *hesed;* so that all that I do, I do as
hesed."

From this point on, wherever he goes, the monk carries
silent devotion with him. His deep prayer of *hesed* flows on
whether he shivers with cold in his sleep, or rests quietly while
he dreams, or wakes into the silence of the day, Someone
inside having watched through the night.

Does this sound strange? Then listen to the Old Testament,
where the psalmist sleeps, while his heart remains awake. And
then listen to a master of the Christian tradition, Isaac of
Syria, who describes how the incense of prayer ascends from
the silence of the heart all the time, so that even in sleep prayer
flows secretly on its course. . . .

* * *

The monk travels, yet never moves. Always on pilgrimage,
the *hasid* asks for no directions. Talk to him, and he will seek
no solutions, no explanations, no answers to "the problem of
life." The Destiny of the Secret One has called him to deepen
his gift of silent devotion, and to sing the song of *Ani ledodi.*

Questions? Little time is left for that. But he will always have time to love you, and to share a little of his silence, and whatever bread he may have, and the rays of the thousand suns that sweep through the sky inside him, and through each new leaf.

But perhaps you—and not he—are the one with the questions.

"Is he hungry, cold?"

Perhaps.

"Full, warm?"

Maybe.

"Neither?"

Perhaps that too.

"Where is he going?"

Further into the sky, and its deep rhythm of love.

"But why him?"

Ask the Rebbe, or the prophet Hosea, who centuries ago heard the Secret One's invitation to join the eternal pattern shared by canyons and molecules and atoms.

The Secret One said: "It is but love's stratagem, thus to lead her out into the wilderness; once there, it shall be all words of comfort. Clad in vineyards that wilderness shall be, . . . a passageway of hope; and a song shall be on her lips. . . ."2

* * *

If silent devotion is real, then one should be able to live it anywhere, at any time, under any circumstances.

Especially under any circumstances.

To sing *Ani ledodi* and still be an inmate of Auschwitz, to live in the midst of suffering and still remain fixed in the Silence of the Secret One as a servant of all—does it sound familiar?

Of course you remember. It happened almost two thousand years ago, in the Middle East. An obscure "monk," always on the move: "You cannot go where I am going . . . unless you flow with the passion inside you, and return to the *hesed* of *yom ehad,* and to the Destiny inside your heart."

He dies suspended between heaven and earth, a *Hasid* placed between two thieves. Eventually he rises from the dead, and after a few weeks ascends into a Sky of Light . . . but not before leaving traces of his fiery footprints on the foreheads of his disciples.

These footprints are still flashing in the dark, on the foreheads of monks who continue to crisscross the earth, living for God and his people.

This monk could be anyone. A friend. An aunt. Your wife. A hermit in the wilderness. Or a monk in his monastery.

It could be you.

Perhaps—without realizing it—your forehead is burning with light. And has been for days, for weeks. Even years.

What then?

Don't ask that Luminous Being—don't ask the Rebbe. He will point you back to yourself, and the clay jug of your heart: a paradise of canyons and pine mountains, and hundreds of millions of stars, each one flowing inside the eternal love pattern of the universe.

As for the Holy Rebbe, you can be sure that he will continue to stand behind your shoulder with his questions: Are you uplifting the world with your words? And giving birth to angels by your deeds?

The questions will continue, far into the silence of the wilderness, and the light of *yom ehad.* They will follow us into the heavens, where Moshe, the old monk Moshe, is still whispering psalms before an open window.

Moshe: having answered all the questions, still singing *Ani ledodi,* still waiting for his fellow pilgrims to dismantle their doubts and soar high into the air like Kazantzakis's archer, as though they'd shot their souls into the sun.

In The Heart of a Great Round Dance

"The further up and further in you go, the bigger everything gets. The inside is larger than the outside."

Lucy looked hard at the garden and saw that it was not really a garden at all but a whole world, with its own rivers and woods and sea and mountains. But they were not strange: she knew them all.

"I see," she said. "This is still Narnia, and more real and more beautiful than the Narnia down below. . . . I see . . . world within world, Narnia within Narnia. . . ."

"Yes," said Mr Tumnus, "like an onion: except that as you continue to go in and in, each circle is larger than the last."

C. S. Lewis

Trees and people have at least this much in common: each is an ecstasy of depth within depth: world within world, Narnia within Narnia.

Right now, heavy snow is covering the pear tree outside my window. Narnia is hiding, waiting for me with its clay jug, its world of rivers and woods and mountains.

But spring is near. Soon the snow will melt, Narnia will appear, and the pear tree's green will break into the sunlight.

Its familiar shape will return: beginning at its outer parts, ending in its inner world, its Narnia within Narnia.

If we could see—in the biblical sense of "experience"—we would see more than the green and branches and pears of this world of Narnia. We would see into layers of depth: molecular, atomic, subatomic. . . . We would see these levels melt into light, and into the silence of infinity: the celestial "sound" of Narnia within Narnia.

If we could see, we would see what philosophers call "being": an intimate depth shared by every pocket of creation. We would experience the level where—according to Bell's Theorem—everything is connected. Today physicists are finding that some unknown force, traveling faster than the speed of light, ties everything together. But to see this force field we have to tiptoe quietly down long flights of stairs, to the "level" where music is flowing out of unseen strings. We have to settle down into the kernel of the tree, where Narnia transcends Narnia.

* * *

If we could see people, we would enjoy the same pattern of beauty and order we find in the tree. At one level we would experience Narnia: senses, thoughts, feelings—all at different layers of depth. At another level we would see the freedom of "this clay jug": the world of "I am," beyond individuality and the sense of "I" and "mine"; a world beyond experience, the spaciousness of all there is, the land of "we."

If we could see, we would see the world of the whole person, with all its parts intersecting like the marvelous upside-down tree of the *Katha Upanisad:* its roots in the heavens. We would see the total sound of Narnia within Narnia, inner plus outer: the antithesis of a *maya*—illusion—which chooses one world (either vertical or horizontal) over the other. We would see total truth, the fragrance of apparently divergent "worlds" intersecting to form the temple of the Great Round Dance.

* * *

The Greek Fathers describe the Trinity as a Round Dance in which Love flames forth from one Person to the Other in a flow that never ceases. Its deep melody carries on night and day inside its Narnia within Narnia—like the orderly and rhythmic process of subatomic particles spinning round and round at immense speed.

This is a love secret, not of three gods but of the One God. The earliest trinitarian formulas never mention the Father, the Son, and the Holy Spirit, but speak only "of the God, the Christ, and the Spirit. Neither the Son nor the Spirit is *God,* but, precisely, the Son of God and the Spirit of God, 'equal' to the One God . . . as God. . . .":[1] the Secret *One.*

The Father is One and his Dance is Three: Love flowing out of the Silence of the Secret One to the Son, and returning to Abba in one concurrent, timeless motion—in the embrace of the Spirit, the "We" of the Father and the Friend.

Dancing back to Abba is the Event of the Holy Spirit, a Wind which sweeps through the silence of the heart: a place which has lived for six thousand years, and sixty times six thousand. And beyond the time when one first heard time.

> Sometimes, when a bird cries out,
> Or the wind sweeps through a tree,
> Or a dog howls in a far off farm,
> I hold still and listen a long time.
>
> My soul turns and goes back to the place
> Where, a thousand forgotten years ago,
> The bird and the blowing wind
> Were like me, and were my brothers.
>
> My soul turns into a tree . . .[2]

The wind of *yom ehad* sweeps the whole tree—the universe

—into the madness—the intensity—of a Friend flowing to his Destiny.

Narnia within Narnia, world within world: Christ is still in the wilderness, with his silence and deep song.

The Tears of an Innocent God

"You're not the same as other women, Mary," the rabbi repeated in a solemn tone, raising his hand as though he wished to prevent all objections. "And your son. . . ."

"My son?" said Mary, her voice trembling. "My son, Father?"

"He is not like other sons, Mary," the rabbi boldly replied.

He weighed his words once more, and continued after a moment. "Sometimes when he is alone during the night and thinks no one is watching him, the whole circumference of his face gleams in the darkness. . . ."

Nikos Kazantzakis

Have you noticed how often "fire" and "light" occur in the literature of religious experience?

In the Bible the Secret One becomes a "consuming fire" who means to refine and purify. God appears to Moses in the burning Bush, and to Elias in a fiery chariot; and when deep shadows sweep through the body of the human race, Christ awakens the fading brightness by bringing "fire" to the world.

Symeon, a saint of the Eastern Orthodox Church, calls the light of God "invisible fire." The Old Testament identifies the

Secret One as the source of this light; while the New Testament calls Christ the "light of the world": the One who shares his love-secret with every pocket of the universe. His joy spreads itself over the world, his light strikes

> . . . the chords of my love:
> the sky opens, the wind runs wild,
> laughter passes over the earth. . . .[1]

The luminous Christ shares the secret of "divine laughter" with his friends in the wilderness. In the silence of the Great Round Dance "the Father laughs to the Son and the Son laughs back to the Father; and this laughter begets liking, and liking begets joy, and joy begets love, and love begets Person, and Person begets the Holy Spirit."[2] In the heart of "invisible fire" the Friend and his Father laugh *to*—and not at—each other. Meister Eckhart's medieval image symbolizes the unceasing forward and backward exchange of life and love in the Great Round Dance.

Right now the Light is striking chords outside my window, in the silence where dawn is breaking and an orphaned fawn is wandering across an open field, hungry and bewildered, looking for a mother he will never find. In a fraction of a second the senses of the Risen Christ will awaken a hermit who has overslept, whose dreams have been the dreams of a Secret Friend watching through the night. The old man will fall to his knees before a cross, and its center gleaming with light. A sentence will float up from inside his world within world, his Narnia within Narnia: "Open my lips, Abba, and my tongue will sing your praise. . . ."

And I will continue to listen to the Apocalypse, and to the Lamb whose face sparkles like jasper and carnelian, the silence whose right hand holds the radiance of seven stars. I will bow down to the Christ of the Apocalypse, the man whose energy is encircled by an emerald-colored rainbow; the God whose loving-kindness throws off sparks of light.

This Christ I bow down to—from inside the "clay jug" of my heart, and from within the Depth of the Great Round Dance—is a being whose humanity and divinity are stitched together, inseparable, like the two poles of the earth. He is the "play" of Gregory Nazianzen's poetry, where luminous fingers stir the cosmos back and forth, round and round, into forms of every kind. The play of the Risen Christ is a fragrance which never sleeps, the energy of the sanskrit *lila*—"play"—a word with roots in *lelay:* to flame, to sparkle, to shine.

Christ is the God of the Apocalypse: the Alpha and the Omega, the Beginning and the End; as well as a man whose humanity began as a tiny light in a barn, surrounded by wise men heavy with sleep, and the barking of dogs in the distance.

> A warm and mild haze
> hung around the trees;
> the moon was going down
> in a west of gold and silk
> like some full and divine womb . . .
> My chest was thumping
> as if my heart were drunk . . .
> I opened the barn door to see if
> He was there.
> He was![3]

* * *

Christ, the man.

Because he is not tied up in his emotions, because he is not entangled in his imagination or locked inside his intellect, because Christ is free, he is the servant of the wilderness. Because he is a man with roots in the heavens and leaves and flowers offering *namasté* to the earth, Christ's silence blossoms into unpredictable shades of feeling: appropriate gestures of a deeply feeling person, each one a response to the concrete world of this wilderness, and the buried gardens of Eboli.

Christ's humanity is no illusion. He is fullness: a life with two sides, each as real as the other. Christ is a being who pervades the universe in the human form of the Risen Christ; but he is also the Invisible Fire who stirs the cosmos at will. His life says that the "monk" is also real: not an angel, or a body, or a mind—but a thinker whose love is incarnate, a servant whose silence blossoms into gestures of authentic emotion: a smile, laughter, tears, a lullaby to a sleepy child. . . .

The experience of other cultures offers the same truth of human balance and wholeness. The Buddha's smile expresses the joy of a man whose breath continually glides in and out of a deep wellspring of silence; the contentment of a human being whose every gesture is a gesture of silence.

> Can a man take fire into his heart,
> and his clothes not burst into flame?[4]

Krishna's ecstatic flute playing marks the intensification of the same joy. His music is human emotion elevated to the highest level, an intensity sweeping out of an ecstatic kernel of light, like the songs of southern Spain which cry out: *Viva Dios!* "Long live God!"

> I love you so much with this curiously alive and
> lonely body . . . With that it loves you madly, beyond
> all rules and conventions, even the six holes in the
> flute move about under the dark man's fingers, and
> the piercing cry goes out over the grown up pastures
> no one sees or visits at dusk except the deer . . .[5]

The gestures of Buddha and Krishna merge into a third

gesture, one which focuses on another flavor of human feeling: the tears of Christ.

In the Gospels Jesus weeps over Jerusalem, and over the death of his friend Lazarus. In each case his tears express the same intensity with which he heals the paralytic, washes the feet of his pupils, returns the boy of Nain to his widowed mother.

Christ's tears flow from and embody the *Kebod Yahweh,* the Shining Glory of Abba. They reach through miles and miles of light to speak of a Friend who watches and cares with intensity. . . .

Christ, the Hasid.

* * *

Jewish tradition calls *hitlahavut* the "burning," the ardor of ecstasy. Listen: "A fiery sword guards the way to the tree of life. It scatters into sparks before the touch of *hitlahavut,* whose light finger is more powerful than it. To *hitlahavut* the path is open, and all bounds sink before its boundless step. The world is no longer its place: it is the place of the world."6

Christ is *hitlahavut* in the wilderness. He is ecstasy in the purest etymological sense: from a Greek word whose roots mean "to stand from." The Greek Fathers describe the Risen Christ as a river flowing from its source (the Father) into the ocean—the Holy Spirit, the bond of the Father and the Son.

Christ is *hitlahavut,* the outpouring of the Secret One. The tears of an Innocent God.

* * *

Uri-Zvi Grinberg in one of his poems describes Christ's appearance in a small village in Eastern Europe. Elie Wiesel paraphrases the poem: "He is looking for his brothers—he is looking for his people. When he does not find them, he asks a passer-by, 'Where are the Jews?'—'Killed,' says the passer-by. 'All of them?—'All of them.'—And their homes?' —'Demolished.'—'Their synagogues?'—'Burned.'—'Their sages?'—'Dead.'—'Their students?'—'Dead too.'—'And their children? What about their children? Dead too?'—'All of them, they are all dead.' And Jesus begins to weep over the slaughter of his people. He weeps so hard that people turn around to look at him, and suddenly one peasant exclaims, 'Hey, look at that, here is another Jew, how did he stay alive?' And the peasants throw themselves on Jesus. . . ."[7]

The tears of Abba disappear from the midst of his people: rejected, unrecognized.

"I am returning to the Secret One who sent me, yet none of you has asked where I am going. . . ."

A Deep Silence vanishes into the sea, leaving behind his fire and his tears.

A Far Green Country

The Baptist filled a deep shell and with trembling hand began to pour water over Jesus' face. "The servant of God is baptized. . . ." he began. But he stopped: he did not know what name to give.

He turned to ask Jesus; but just as everyone, stretched on tiptoe, expected to hear the name, wings were heard to descend from the heavens and a white-feathered bird —was it a bird, or one of Jehovah's Seraphim?—darted forward and balanced itself on the head of the baptized. It remained motionless for several moments, then suddenly circled three times above him. Three wreaths of light glowed in the air and the bird uttered a cry as though proclaiming a hidden name, a name never heard before. The heavens seemed to be answering the Baptist's mute question. . . .

He raised his eyes. The bird had already bounded toward the summit of the heavens and become light within the light.

The Baptist, whose years in the desert . . . had enabled him to master the language of God, . . . understood.

Nikos Kazantzakis

As a child, Nikos Kazantzakis was terrified by the thought of Abraham, the great pilgrim of the Old Testament. The first time he heard the name he was appalled: "Those two *ah's* reverberated inside me; they seemed to come from far away, out of some deep, dark, and dangerous well. I whispered 'Abraham, Abraham' secretly to myself and heard footsteps and panting behind me—someone with huge bare feet was pursuing me. . . ."[1] Kazantzakis would hide behind his desk for fear that Abraham would catch him and whisk him off someplace, who knows where. . . .

But to make matters worse, his teacher said, "Just keep the commandments, lads, and you're sure to go to Abraham's bosom." That was enough to convince Kazantzakis that he must never, never keep the commandments.

But there is an element of truth in Kazantzakis's description of Abraham. The sound of his name did flow from far away, as though from some deep well: the silence of the Secret One.

Hebrew tradition identifies one's whole person with the name, so when the Secret One changed Abram's name to Abraham, it marked a turning point in the old man's life: his surrender to a Secret Destiny. It meant that he was ready to go even into the unknown reaches of a wilderness where, like John the Baptist, centuries later, he would learn the language of God. Abraham was seventy-five when his Secret Friend asked him to leave his country and his kinfolk and his father's home.

But the paradox of *hitlahavut* is this: by asking Abraham to "leave," the Secret One was asking him to "stay"; to remain with his kinfolk and his friends—in the silence and love of "this clay jug," and the massive waters that burn in the wilderness.

"I'm calling you to live," the Secret One was saying. "I'm inviting you to experience your friends and your God at a level beyond words, or concepts, or feelings; and at the same time to express that living through words and concepts and feelings. Do you understand, Abraham, my brother? The kernel and its shell, together. The journey of *hitlahavut* is not a flight from, or an escape to, but a return to an ancient gift. 'Leaving' is like a tree waking up after sleeping for millions of years, crying out in amazement after seeing itself for the first time: fresh green shoots, strong leaves, deep roots, thick branches, hundreds and millions of almonds, even in winter. . . .

"In receiving this gift the pilgrim awakens; he comes to his senses. The Secret One teaches him the language of paradise, and the sound of creation. He learns to laugh—in the Friend, to the Father. He masters the language of the Father laughing back to, not at—the pilgrim in the Friend. You will understand this as you move deeper into the journey, Abraham."

* * *

Beginning with Abraham, "the father of believers," a pattern emerges: a consistent rhythm of pilgrimage. In the next generation, Isaac leaves his mother, and after him, Jacob leaves Beersheba. In the next generation, Joseph leaves for Egypt, and after him Moses leaves Egypt and leads the Jewish people into the wilderness.

> Then Frodo kissed Merry and Pippin, and last of all Sam, and went aboard; and the sails were drawn up, and the wind blew, and slowly the ship slipped away down the long grey firth; and the light of the glass of Galadriel that Frodo bore glimmered and was lost. And the ship went out into the High Sea and passed on into the West, until at last on a night of rain Frodo smelled a sweet fragrance on the air and heard the sound of singing that came over the water. And then it seemed to him that . . . the grey rain-curtain turned all to silver glass and was rolled back, and he beheld white shores and beyond them a far green country under a swift sunrise.[2]

The pattern continues. The exodus goes on, as one by one pilgrims leave for the gift of *hitlahavut,* and the sweet fragrance on the air, and the sound of singing over the water, and the wind that carries the monk's tears into the blind trees of Eboli.

One by one the prophets are sent away into the darkness of unknown lands, to roll away a brooding curtain of rain, and change heavy shadows into silver glass. One by one they leave, with gladness and deep song: Isaias, Baruch, Ezechiel, Daniel, Hosea. . . .

And Habacuc.

We know little about Habacuc—only that his name derives from a word meaning "fruit tree," or "plant," and that he was asked to go on a mission to Daniel in the lion's den. His contribution to the Old Testament is minimal, if we judge in terms of length: Habacuc's prophecy fills barely a couple of pages.

His best known aphorism: "We live by faith"—the way a plant lives by the sap that flows through its stalk, and the way Christ lives in the wilderness: by the waters that flow through the rocks, the *hitlahavut* of his beloved Abba.

Habacuc was another Old Testament figure whose imaginary presence terrified Nikos Kazantzakis as a child. When the writer first heard the prophet's name in grammar school, he reacted as vehemently as he had to the "specter" of Abraham. Responding to inner fantasies, the child was sure that Habacuc was a "bogeyman," prowling around in the shadows of the courtyard at night. In *Report to Greco,* Kazantzakis recalls an "incident" in which, after summoning up all his courage, he goes to the courtyard alone at night. Suddenly "the prophet" leaps up from behind a well, thrusts out a hand and yells: *Habacuc!*

But as in his delusions about Abraham, even this description of Habacuc holds some truth.

The shadows in the courtyard are real: but they are not the cloak of Habacuc prowling around in the moonlight. "Yahweh is our shadow,"[3] a spiritual master says somewhere: the Secret One pursues us everywhere, whether we walk or eat—

or run, like a child fleeing from the hand of an imaginary prophet.

When Habacuc says, "we live by faith," he is talking about a surrender to an Invisible Presence: a yielding to a Gentle Hand that flows out of a deep wellspring of Silent Devotion, to ignite and transform the heart of the pilgrim into the white shores of *hitlahavut,* and the passion of a far green country.

Habacuc's faith is an even vision that sees the Invisible Hand of *hitlahavut* behind every circumstance and event. Faith is *'aman*—"firm, solid"—and *'emet*—"fidelity," the sister of *hesed:* the love-energy promised by the Secret One to "the father of believers," the holy pilgrim Abraham.

Habacuc's faith is the "madness" behind the pilgrim's dance into the High Sea, the wholeness that unfolds when the sails are drawn up, and the wind blows, and the ship steals down the long grey firth. It is the sanity that dawns when the ship passes on into the West, and turns its back on the grey and brooding rain-curtain that hides the radiance of a swift sunrise, and the white shores of a far green country.

Faith is a sanity that celebrates in the midst of all circumstances, an innocence that knows no brooding—like St. Paul, who knew that nothing—hardship, hunger, death—could separate him from the love of the Christ who had led him into the wilderness.

The pilgrim's faith is the sanity of a vision that sees with intensity: a certitude that knows that the rocks of the wilderness are more than rocks, and hobbits more than hobbits, and the kernel of life more than its shell.

Faith is more than an emotional or intellectual assent to Mystery. It is Christ stretching out his hand to Peter in the storm, and Peter seeing Christ, and surrendering to the hand. Faith is Peter yielding to *tarnar,* the Indian word for "savior," which literally means one who "causes us to float."

Faith is a surrender that flows from the silence of deep

roots, and climbs into the branches and leaves, and expands into the fruit and flowers of the tree.

Faith is the wholeness of silent devotion.

The Journey

"One must assume responsibility for being in a weird world," he said. "We are in a weird world, you know."

I nodded my head affirmatively.

"We're not talking about the same thing," he said. "For you the world is weird because if you're not bored with it you're at odds with it. For me the world is weird because it is stupendous, awesome, mysterious, unfathomable; my interest has been to convince you that you must assume responsibility for being here, in this marvelous world, in this marvelous desert, in this marvelous time. I wanted to convince you that you must learn to make every act count, since you are going to be here for only a short while, in fact, too short for witnessing all the marvels of it."

Carlos Castaneda

A Hasidic tale describes a pilgrim trapped in the darkness of loneliness and fear. Rebbe Barukh seeks out his young disciple and says: "My son, you started out with a question. And found the answer—which enabled you to open the first gate of reason. Then you leaped to a second question, and the same thing happened. A second gate opened, and you passed through. Then you ran to another gate, and another: all the time following the same pattern of question, struggle, solution, passage. And now you are staring at the fiftieth gate—and you are terrified. Why? Because you know that if you fling open the gate, you will have to deal with a question beyond your control, a question no human can ask, and an answer no human can fathom."

The young man begins to tremble: What is he to do? Go back to the second gate?

Rebbe Barukh shakes his head.

"No," he says, "You can never go back."

"Why not? Why can't I go back? What else is there to do?"

"Keep your rendezvous with what is beyond the fifty gates of reason—that is what else there is to do, my son. Let your gaze go forward. Surrendering is not as frightening as you think: it's very natural. You think darkness is lurking out there, hovering beyond the entrance to the fiftieth gate: a darkness that you feel will swallow you up.

"Wrong. Darkness is not what awaits you, but light. . . . Open the gate—better, let it open for you—and you will find the tender hand of faith. Do you understand, my son? Faith has been expecting you, like a woman awaiting her beloved after a long voyage at sea."

The young man leaves. He opens the gate, and returns to the white shores of silence and love, and the ecstatic waters of *hitlahavut*.

Beyond the fiftieth gate, the sound of *Ani ledodi*.

* * *

Faith transcends question and answer; it leaps beyond the fifty gates of reason—and the boundaries of the senses, the imagination, the emotions, the intellect. And yet, at the same time, faith includes these elements: as the kernel includes its shell.

Both kernel and shell comprise the whole person. They are the place of faith; but better still is to expand into the vision of the Witness who watches without judging. Faith is the Friend looking out from the eyes of a heart that has always seen, without realizing that it was seeing.

But first one must embrace the emptiness of "this clay jug," walk to an Open Hand, and regain the gift of sight.

* * *

The vision of faith is the ecstasy of experience: a deep seeing into the language of *hitlahavut.*

All that the pilgrim sees through the eyes of faith is "context"—in the etymological sense of "what is woven together," in the cycle of the Great Round Dance.

That is why all things matter to the pilgrim: he knows that everything is the language of God. He sees—and receives— each event as a gift from an Invisible Hand, a fragment of a plan conceived by a Secret Friend in what the Sufis call *azaliat* —"outside of historical time"—so that gradually all of the pilgrim's life becomes a continuous eucharist of the heart: a perpetual conceiving of the love of the Secret One in "this clay jug," which yields its soil to the harvest of God's Delight, his Joy, his Peace, his Rest.

To see this way is to "take on the mind of Christ": *eucharistia,* gratitude. A "madness" which celebrates in the garden of this wilderness, in every season:

How marvelous is that garden, where apples and pears, both for the sake of the the two Marys, are arriving even in winter.

Those apples grow from the Gift, and they sink back into the Gift.

It must be that they are coming from the garden to the garden.[1]

* * *

Abraham and his descendants were filled with this life of gratitude, this outpouring of faith we find so often in the psalms of David.

The pattern of leaving begun by Abraham in the Old Testament—an exodus into *eucharistia*—flows into the pages of the New Testament, where Peter and Andrew leave their nets, James and John their father Zebedee. . . .

A teacher sits beneath the shade of an almond tree, giving his pupils instructions for a journey.

"You won't need a traveling bag or staff."

"What about sandals?"

"Not even that."

"But we'll need money—and bread for the journey."

"Money and bread, when you have the wind and the sky? But there is one other thing that I want you to leave behind."

"What is that?"

"Your doubts."

So the pupils leave—without provisions—or doubts. Poor, all of them: poured out—like Abraham and Habacuc. Empty as the hollow in the reed of Krishna's flute, "the narrow riftless emptiness which can have only one destiny: to receive the piper's breath and to utter the song that is in his heart."[2]

The call to pilgrimage is a call to poverty, and therefore to purity of heart.

"If your heart is pure, you will see the Secret One."

"Pure" means unmixed, uncluttered. But to manipulate, to covet, to grasp—all this is to clutter "this clay jug" with alien water, and to jam the hollow of the reed with something other than the Song of the Secret One.

The emptiness of the pilgrim is the other side of fullness: a vast sky without clouds. The pilgrim becomes this fullness—*pleroma*—in proportion to the depth of his *kenosis:* the emptying out of whatever blocks his awareness of a prayer that goes on inside his heart without ceasing.

The prayer of *Ani ledodi,* sung from the depths of the Great Round Dance.

* * *

Sometimes the call to emptiness can involve a radical form

of pilgrimage—the surrender of all "identification": security, title, function, place in society, home.

Senseless? Unproductive?

No matter. When the Secret One whispers his call to the wilderness, the pilgrim leaves everything and takes to the road—even if it means "death" to stability of the outer kind.

And why not?

The Divine Rebbe has set the example. He has no title, no name, no function in society. What he does often seems senseless. He has no home, is not established, is "nobody." He roams from place to place, standing behind shoulders with his questions: "Are you uplifting the world with your words? Are you giving birth to angels by your deeds?"

What else is there to do, but follow the example of the Luminous Rebbe and the holy pilgrim Abraham. . . .

> I gave orders for my horse to be brought round from the stable. The servant did not understand me. I myself went to the stable, saddled my horse and mounted. In the distance I heard a bugle call. I asked him what this meant. He knew nothing and had heard nothing. At the gate he stopped me, asking: "Where are you riding to, master?" "I don't know," I said, "only away from here, away from here. Always away from here, only by doing so can I reach my destination." "And so you know your destination?" he asked. "Yes," I answered, "didn't I say so? Away-From-Here, that is my destination." "You have no provisions with you," he said. "I need none," I said, "the journey is so long that I must die of hunger if I don't get anything on the way. No provisions can save me. For it is, fortunately, a truly immense journey."[3]

You are on your journey when one day you find yourself in a conference room where a monk is giving a talk about a man who enters a monastery . . . and what happens after that.

The first time he enters, things don't work out—so he leaves and goes to another monastery for a while. When that doesn't work out, he leaves and gets a job. But that doesn't work out either. So he returns to the monastery . . . and then leaves to become a hermit. But he comes out of that life-style, too.

Nothing works: nothing seems to fit. Yet all the time he is saying "yes" to the Rebbe, from the silence of a heart which keeps growing in emptiness and blossoming into the maturity of faith.

"And then he went to Paris."

You lean forward intently, eager for the monk to go on.

"And then he went to Paris and worked with the poor. And then, one day. . . ."

The monk's voice trails off almost into a whisper.

"He just died."

Silence.

The monk says it again, in a whisper.

"He just died."

A wall collapses inside you, and you sit, numb.

And the Almond Tree Blossomed

We had toured the Holy Mountain for forty days. When, completing our circle, we finally returned to Daphne, the most unexpected, most decisive miracle was awaiting us. Though it was the heart of winter, there in a small, humble orchard was an almond tree in bloom!

Seizing my friend's arm, I pointed to the blossoming tree.

"Angelos," I said, "during the whole of this pilgrimage our hearts have been tormented by many intricate questions. Now, behold the answer!"

My friend riveted his blue eyes upon the flowering almond tree and crossed himself, as though doing obeisance before a holy wonder-working icon. He remained speechless for a long moment. Then, speaking slowly, he said, "A poem is rising to my lips, a tiny little poem: a haiku."

He looked again at the almond tree.

> I said to the almond tree,
> "Sister, speak to me of God."
> And the almond tree blossomed.
>
> *Nikos Kazantzakis*

Sometimes the first stages of "seeing" can be as overwhelming as the experience of Bob Edens, who just regained his eyesight after fifty-one years of darkness. Bob is amazed by what he has seen so far: the shape of the moon, a jet plane leaving a trail of vapor across the sky, the purple and orange in the face of a tiger . . . and *yellow!* Bob can find no words to describe the ecstasy of seeing *yellow.*

"And did I mention," he says, "that I saw a leaf drifting through the air, like it has a mind of its own?"

But sometimes the first stages of seeing are not so overwhelming. Faith unfolds quietly, smoothly—so much so that one is tempted to say: "Nothing is happening."

But a tree doesn't "happen."

It just blossoms.

* * *

The gift of faith grows slowly and steadily in the pilgrim heart—much in the way Albert Einstein describes the creative process. When you create a new theory, he says, it's not like putting up a skyscraper in place of an old barn. But rather, it's akin to climbing a high mountain, seeing from a fresh and broader perspective, and finding links everywhere.

"Links everywhere": sparks that ignite gratitude, and impel the pilgrim deeper into the Silent Devotion of the Friend who waits for more pilgrims to pass beyond the fiftieth gate.

* * *

At more advanced stages of the journey, the pilgrim's faith —his seeing—resembles the poetry of Don Luis de Góngora.

Góngora was a master at pulling together the most diverse elements in his poems: calm oceans, hurricane winds. . . . In one poem, he weaves together the sun, the ocean, and a boy's wet clothes, and has the head of a star sip "the least wave . . . from the smallest thread."[1]

Like Góngora, Christ weaves together diverse elements in his own poetry: the verse he sings and shares with the pilgrim in the wilderness.

The Gospels describe this song of Narnia within Narnia,

otherness within oneness. John—the brother of the Friend—states the paradox in the opening lines of his Gospel.

"The Word lived in the beginning"—in the sense of the Sufi *azaliat:* outside of historical time. "And the Word was with God, and the Word was God."

Christ, the Word was—is—God. And yet the Word is other: he is with God. While maintaining oneness with Abba—in the silence of nonduality, beyond "I" or "Thou"—Christ remains a Person who relates *to* the Secret One. Throughout the Gospels we find sparks of love flowing constantly from Christ to the heart of Abba.

At deeper levels of faith, the pilgrim comes to share this paradox of the Risen Christ. The Friend says: "The Father and I are one." And the pilgrim know this is true, because he *sees* that it is true.

But because he looks out from within the depth of Christ, he also sees the other side of this oneness: innumerable shades of light flowing out of silence, as the Father calls the Son—and the pilgrim in the Son—to Himself. And the pilgrim sees the Son responding—by surrendering himself, and the pilgrim, into the arms of Abba.

Christ is one with the Father, and at the same time he thinks of Abba, serves him, speaks of him to others.

So does the pilgrim.

With this one difference: he does not do it as well.

* * *

"I know you're an American, but you seem like one of us—European," a German tells me today. His observation doesn't surprise me. My father was a diplomat from the Walloon region of Belgium, and my mother a gifted pianist from a long line of Andalusian families. So the old châteaus along the Meuse and the snowy trees of the Ardennes forest and the canal of Bruges are all part of me—and so is the poetry of Lorca, and the gypsy music of southern Spain.

Part of my European heritage is *canto hondo:* deep song.

Canto hondo is the ancient music of Andalusia—deeper, Lorca says, than all the wells and seas that surround the world, music so old that "it comes from the first sob and the first kiss."[2] *Canto hondo* is ecstatic, the joy of the Andalusian who rarely notices the "middle tone," who either "shouts at the stars or kisses the red dust of the road. . . ."[3]

Like *canto hondo,* the pilgrim's deep song of faith—a melody he shares with his Secret Friend—is a stranger to the restraint of the "middle tone." A canticle of devotion more ancient than *canto hondo,* it begins beyond time in *azaliat,* in the silence of the Father.

If Christ is the *hitlahavut* of the Father—as a river streaming from its source—then the pilgrim is the *hitlahavut* of Christ.

The love that is deep song begins in the silence of the Father, flows into the Son, and streams into the *cantaor*—the singer. From the pilgrim-*cantaor* love continues its journey, streaming into the deep valleys of the universe, far into the shores of the men and women of this world—all for no other reason than this: "I sing because I sing."

Like *canto hondo,* the pilgrim's deep song "rouses ancient essences from their sleep, wraps them in his voice, and flings them into the wind."[4] The pilgrim *cantaor* is a muse who rouses the buried gardens of Eboli, folds them in his voice, and yields them to the gentle wind of *yom ehad.*

But each *cantaor* rouses ancient essences in his own way— according to the unique gift of his calling to the wilderness: "A tree gives glory to God by being a tree. For in being what God means it to be it is obeying Him. It 'consents,' so to speak, to His creative love. It is expressing an idea which is in God and which is not distinct from the essence of God, and therefore a tree imitates God by being a tree. . . .[5]

> This particular tree will give glory to God by spreading out its roots in the earth and raising its branches into the

air and the light in a way that no other tree before or
after it ever did or will do. . . .[6]

The author of these lines is Thomas Merton: monk, hermit,
poet, writer—a unique *cantaor,* who responded to the gift of
pilgrimage:

> I hear [God] saying to me: "I will . . . lead you into
> solitude. I will lead you by the way that you cannot
> possibly understand, because I want it to be the quickest
> way. . . .
> . . . I shall lead you into the high places of my joy and
> you shall . . . find all things in My mercy, which has
> created you for this end and brought you from Prades to
> Bermuda to St. Antonin to Oakham to London to Cam-
> bridge to Rome to New York to Columbia to Corpus
> Christi to St. Bonaventure to the Cistercian Abbey of the
> poor men who labor in Gethsemani:
> "That you may become the brother of God and learn
> to know the Christ of the burnt men."[7]

Merton died in a hotel room in Bangkok, after sharing his
vision with monks from around the world—a *cantaor* who
gave to the very end.

* * *

We are in the middle of Lent, and on two consecutive days
Christ has ended the Gospel at Mass on the same note: "I have
come here to serve." He will say the same thing in a few weeks,
on Holy Thursday. Christ will kneel and wash the feet of his
disciples, and then the Servant will stand up and look at each
of us for a long, long moment before saying: "I want you to
do the same thing. I want you to pour your tears of *hitlahavut*
into service. I want you to uplift the world with your words,
and give birth to angels by your deeds. I want you to be
cantaors of a vast night full of stars, where the tears of blind
trees can fall at last. . . ."

But the hermit in the wilderness, someone will say—how can he be a *cantaor*? Far from everyone but the silence of the eider duck sitting on her nest—how can he serve?

Listen:

> He who celebrates alone in the heart
>   of the wilderness,
> He is a great assembly.
> If two together celebrate among the rocks,
> Thousands and tens of thousands are present there.
> If three are gathered together,
> A fourth is among them.
> If there are six or seven together,
> Twelve thousand thousand are assembled.
> If they range themselves in rank,
> They fill the firmament with prayer . . .
> When they end their prayer,
> The Lord rises to serve his servants.[8]

* * *

When the Baal Shem Tov saw that his people were in danger, he did not rush to the market place to comfort them. Instead, he went deep into the forest alone and meditated. Then he lit a fire and said a blessing.

And the danger passed over his people, like clouds swept away by the wind, and they lived on and grew in deep faith, like Abraham and Habacuc.

Which is why the hermit can uplift the world without saying a word, and give birth to angels without doing a thing.

Jonas

The Voice of God is heard in Paradise:
"I have always overshadowed Jonas with My mercy
. . .
Have you had sight of Me, Jonas My child?
Mercy within mercy within mercy. . . ."

Thomas Merton

Let me tell you about a *cantaor* named Jonas.

What I know of his early life is rumor: he went AWOL in the Spanish-American War, traveled in Europe, worked for a while, and then—at some point, no one knows exactly when—surrendered to an Invisible Hand.

Jonas entered the Cistercian monastery at Valley Falls, Rhode Island, where he learned the ancient Trappist sign language and took care of the mules and worked around the farm. His life was ordinary—in the dictionary sense of "not remarkable, occurring in the usual course of events." Ordinary, the way the almond tree is ordinary, living its life as part of the "usual course of events": starting as a tiny seed, growing into roots and branches and leaves, finally emerging into a likeness of God that blossoms even in winter.

Brother Jonas was a very ordinary *cantaor*.

> I was welcomed [to the monastery] and allowed to live with the brothers and partake of food with them and be

quiet. The most powerful moment I had was standing in line washing my cup and plate. It was a silent gathering, the seven [worship services] and silence otherwise. I was standing in line behind a brother, and he had the plate in his hand and in the other hand he had the brush with the soap on it, and he was brushing his dish. I whispered to him (we could whisper in the line), "Brother, how long have you been here?" And he said, "Sixteen years." And the image I have is the brush going around in the dish and "Sixteen years." And the way in which he said it. There was no pride . . . no pity . . . no sense of accomplishment. It was merely a statement: "Sixteen years. . . ."[1]

One day the monastery at "the Valley" burned down and Jonas was sent to a new foundation in the Shenandoah Valley. But he always promised that he would return to "the Valley" when the time was right.

Shenandoah summers passed, one after another, and fall days spent picking corn in the rain, and winters awake among the silent rocks, and every spring, the same scripture reading at the Paschal Vigil: "On day one God made the heavens and the earth, a wilderness without form. . . ."

And Jonas came to know the sound of the Great Blue Heron, and the secret of *yom ehad,* and the language of the rocks in the wilderness. He learned how good it is to live in the garden where apples and pears, for his sake, arrived even in winter: growing from the Gift, returning to the Gift. Jonas grew in faith, wisdom, and gratitude. And all the while he knew that his life was touching people he would never see: the way each unique cell contributes to the growth of the whole body of the Risen Christ.

One day Jonas was splitting rocks with a sledgehammer. Drenched with perspiration, he looked up at the sun and made a sign: "hot." He was ninety-five years old.

Later that day he disappeared.

The brothers scattered in different directions, trying to find him: silo, woods, down by the river, the guesthouse, the barn near the orchard grass.

No luck. He wasn't around.

Two brothers got an idea. They took a truck and drove out to the broad highway leading north, to Washington, and eventually to New England. Not far from the monastery they saw someone walking along the road, wearing a straw hat and brown work robes.

They stopped the truck and one of the brothers asked, "Where were you going, Brother?"

"To the Valley," Jonas said, his voice trailing off into a whisper. "I was going back to the Valley. . . ."

A few days later, he went into the infirmary. He said he wasn't feeling well.

In those days, on the eve of the Second Vatican Council, it was the Cistercian custom to ring the bell softly, every few seconds or so, while the priest chanted the Preface of the Mass. When the monastic community left the church one morning, the abbot made a sign: "Go to the infirmary."

Too late.

Brother Jonas had died at the moment when the bell was ringing and the monks would have been singing "Blessed is He Who comes in the name of the Lord. Hosanna in the highest. . . ."

His memorial card carried these lines, found on a piece of paper next to his bed, written minutes before Mass had begun:

> My heart has traveled round the world and found none like Him; whom does He resemble? Whom does He resemble?
>
> Ah, silence! For without speech He gives to all of this wine to taste, He gives to taste, He gives to taste, He gives to taste.[2]

The words of Rumi, another *cantaor* from another age.

My Friends the Friendless

Baptized in the rivers of night, Gethsemani has recovered her innocence. Darkness brings a semblance of order before all things disappear. With the clock slung over my shoulder, in the silence of the Fourth of July, it is my time to be the night watchman, in the house that will one day perish. . . .

The church. In spite of the stillness, the huge place seems alive. Shadows move everywhere, around the small uncertain area of light which the sanctuary light casts on the Gospel side of the altar. There are faint sounds in the darkness, the empty choir-stalls creak and hidden boards mysteriously sigh. . . .

Here, in this place where I made my vows, where I had my hands anointed for the Holy Sacrifice, where I have had Your priesthood seal the depth and intimate summit of my being, a word, a thought, would defile the quiet of Your inexplicable love. . . .

Thomas Merton

Deep inside the night, I leave the farmhouse where no one is sleeping. I move slowly past the heavy shadows in the bullpen: restless, even at this hour. He must be the bull who got into the barn before dawn yesterday, while the sisters were milking the cows. (Pandemonium: nuns scattering in every direction,

some of them running to the chaplain's house for help.
. . .)

Now I am in the clearing. Ahead of me is the monastic
church: silhouetted against the sky, under the full moon, between two stars. This is the sacred place the desert fathers
called a "festive hall": the house of prayer where "singers"
meet to celebrate their communal gift of inner monasticism.
This is the Holy of Holies, the tent in the wilderness where
Abraham sang psalms to the Secret One long before David
was born. This is the sanctuary where monks dance the dance
of No One.

In this festive hall, where the community of faith begins to
gather in the darkness hours before dawn, nobody is "one":
in the sense of an individual "one" pitted against other individual "ones." Here, to be "No One" is to be "one" in the
purest sense: one with oneself, others, creation, the Secret
One.

I draw near the church door, turn the knob, and step in.

And kneel into miles and miles of quiet, and the No One
of *yom ehad.*

* * *

The church—attached to the Cistercian convent—reminds
me of the chapel at Mt. Saviour, a Benedictine monastery in
upstate New York. Both of them express the simplicity of
monos: one.

I remember hearing about a symposium held at Mt. Saviour
ten years ago, attended by Hindus, Christians, Buddhists,
Muslims: an assembly of No One. Let me tell you how it
ended.

The final words of the symposium spoken, the participants
leave for the chapel, passing through two lines: their hosts, the
monks. The passage is a ritual of mutual *namasté,* carried out
in silence.

The chapel. Here the altar is in the middle of this sacred
place: everything converges on that focal point, everything

flows from its center. It is a rock shining in the midst of the wilderness, like the brilliant body described by a Japanese *roshi* at the symposium: "I am a zen *bonze.* I have been ten years in the United States, but I still can't speak English. I feel I am shaking hands with you wearing gloves. . . . My body is 65 years old, but it has its own incomparable brilliance; it is a unique body. . . . However, I do not mean that you do not have your own brilliant and unique bodies . . . While each of us has the common brilliance of being a human being, there is a unique individuality and distinction. . . ."[1]

A brilliant body with a hundred trillion cells: the assembly of No One.

Now that everyone is in the chapel, the four double doors are opened: each one facing a different corner of the universe. A monk rings the bell: slowly, solemnly. Its deep sound floats over the hills of the countryside, and beyond the treetops of the forest, to the four ends of this world—and its world within world, its Narnia within Narnia.

No psalms, no reading, no song: the bell is the sole canticle of this assembly of No One.

Now, each in his own time, the pilgrims rise up from their places and leave through one of the four doors of the festive hall. . . .

* * *

Like Mount Saviour, the altar—and its tabernacle—is the axis of this place of festive innocence. Its sacred hands reach out to touch every visitor, every stranger—and turn him into a friend, no stranger. The altar knows no distinctions: guests with shoes, guests without shoes, religious, irreligious. . . . No fingerprints, no badges. Monks, everyone. No one at all.

> My friends without fathers or houses hear
> Doors opening in the darkness . . .
> My friends without keys go out from jails
> it is night. . . .[2]

The road to this Cistercian church has been a long one for these friends of mine, with all those years behind a curtain of mist, their eyes locked inside deep walls.

They remind me of a man I've been reading about in Elie Wiesel's *The Gates of the Forest:* [3] Gregor, a survivor of a concentration camp. Midway through the book he challenges a Rebbe: "After Auschwitz, how can you still believe in God?"

The Rebbe's answer: "After Auschwitz, how can you *not* believe in God?"

Some time later, Gregor, now conscious of the tears that have gathered in his chest over the years, returns to the Hasidic master.

"Rebbe," Gregor pleads, "make me able to weep."

"Not enough," the Rebbe says. "Tears are not enough. I will teach you how to sing."

* * *

Suddenly, out of the deep silence, the hand of this festive hall reaches out like the Rebbe, and taps the shoulder of one of my friends—the one with the trim black beard, staring at the altar.

"May I ask you something?"

"Of course."

"Why are you here?"

"Why do you ask? Do you want us to leave?"

"Not at all. You're very welcome here. Do you mind if I ask what you're thinking about?"

"This place—its silence, its simplicity. The four doors opening out to the world. I feel uneasy here, and yet . . . it's. . . ."

"Your house."

"May I ask you a favor?"

"Certainly."

"Speak plainly. Otherwise you make me suspicious."

"I would be suspicious too, if I came off the road you have been traveling these long years."

"So you know that we are drifters?"

"And soon you will be pilgrims."

"I asked you to speak plainly. You're ridiculing us. It's bad manners for the host to ridicule his guests. But we're accustomed to this kind of treatment."

"I didn't mean to offend you. I was speaking the truth."

"What do you mean, pilgrims? Something religious?"

"Stick around a while. You'll see."

"You listen well. I'm curious."

"It's not enough to be curious. You have to sing—and dance. You must, it's easy to celebrate. It's natural to be No One. . . ."

Suddenly, in the silence of this House of prayer, a wall of darkness gets up and moves. It opens the roof, darts into the sky and disappears with a sharp click—like an umbrella closing in the middle of the night. Off in the distance, a grandfather clock strikes four times.

One by one my friends fall quietly to their knees and close their eyes. They listen, my friends without keys, my friends from jails—to the light of the Great Blue Heron echoing off the highway. They kneel, my friends without fathers or houses, into the light of *yom ehad* far within, and the sound of sails drawn up, and the silence of a ship sailing away down a long grey firth.

My friends, the pilgrims.

* * *

A bell tinkles down a long corridor far away, inside the cloister. It draws closer, closer. . . .

The nuns rise up from the shadows out there, take their places in the choir stalls, and face the altar and its tabernacle.

The lights—soft and gentle—go on.

Lauds begins.

The nuns bow, stand, sing, sit—and listen, waiting for the

Word of the Secret One to descend into their hearts. Then they stand again with grateful faces, and chant—slowly, to a deep rhythm of psalmody—and sing, and bow again.

One rhythm, one song: the nuns, my friends and I, flowing together inside another rhythm, another unseen song: the Love Canticle of the Great *Cantaor.*

> What concert is it, that the soul spins
> round dancing?
> What whistle is it, that
> the heart is coming flapping wings?
> What a marriage feast it is! What a wedding! . . .[4]

Deep inside the night, the festive sound of *Ani ledodi.*

* * *

Lauds is over.

All the lights go off, except for one: shining over the altar, above the tabernacle. Slowly, the old chaplain carries the Blessed Sacrament from the silence of the tabernacle and puts it in a vessel on the altar, where it will remain for half an hour.

Now all you see—out of—is that eucharistic presence on top of the wooden altar. Nothing else. And yet you do see everything else, encircling that Host like so many spokes of a wheel.

Everyone is in the Host: my friends, the chaplain, the bull, the cows, the barn, the nuns with nothing to leave behind, except memories of silence and love.

Nothing, but No One.

* * *

Dawn.

The eucharistic celebration begins.

The Sky opens: Abba calls. The still surface of Christ-water sparkles into wave after wave of Endless Kindness, glinting off the surface of the earth, coursing back to the Silence of the Secret One.

Abba rejoices and embraces the Son, in the "We" of the Blessed Spirit: the strong wind of *yom ehad*.

Now we—bulls, nuns, chaplain, barn, my friends and I—all within the heart of Christ the Sea, receive back Abba's Love on this eucharistic tide . . . all from within the Center of the universe, shining from that tiny altar cloth.

Now it is time to flow back again on this tide: along with fields full of flowers and the buried light of Eboli, and the silence of the eider duck sitting on her nest.

A climate of *eucharistia*—gratitude—pervades the festive hall, and expands beyond the windows of its sacred precincts.

> . . . My thankfulness flies out over the water like fragments of lightning, or a beam broken up into sparks.
>
> All at once I understand the virgin and her candles, and I understand the great gray body of the whale rolling in the sea, with his sides glistening, and I understand why my hair is up near the clouds . . .[5]

In the Sky, where it belongs, from which it came, to which it is returning.

All the time, inside fiery tears, and a wind which never ceases.

* * *

Now, the joy of sharing: the symbolic kiss of peace, and the truth that "in the plan of the Great Dance plans without number interlock, and each movement becomes in its season the breaking into flower of the whole design to which all else had been directed. Thus each is equally at the centre and none are there by being equals, but some by giving place and some by receiving it, the small things by their smallness and the great by their greatness, and all the patterns linked and looped together by the unions of a kneeling with a sceptred love. Blessed be He."[6]

Now everyone approaches the table to share the eucharistic meal. The Secret One runs to meet us. . . .

> A caravan of sugar has arrived from Egypt; the sound of footfall and bells is coming.
> Ha, be silent, for to complete the ode our speaking King is coming.[7]

Silence, peace. The sound of tiny birds in the treetops. The Liturgy has ended.
We are No One.

* * *

Precisely thirty minutes after the end of Mass, a door opens. A smiling nun with long, angular features—an open face—glides into the hall and tells us, in Cistercian sign language, that we have to leave: she has to clean the church.

We understand, and leave.

As we open the door, one of my friends leans over and whispers the supreme compliment in my ear: "*Es de buena familia.*" "She comes from a good family."

We step out of the front door into an endless hall, as long as the edge of the Heron's wing. It leads down a long grey firth, into an open sea. . . .

Suddenly I wake up into bright sunlight, and the sound of the wind moving through the wheeling stars: thrown out of paradise once more, back on the road again, my book still open at the passage where Odysseus rescues his friends by giving his name as *No One.*

Dabar

For the world and time are the dance of the Lord in emptiness. The silence of the spheres is the music of a wedding feast. The more we persist in misunderstanding the phenomena of life, the more we analyze them out into strange finalities and complex purposes of our own, the more we involve ourselves in sadness, absurdity and despair. But it does not matter much, because no despair of ours can alter the reality of things, or stain the joy of the cosmic dance which is always there. . . .

Yet the fact remains that we are invited to forget ourselves on purpose, cast our awful solemnity to the winds and join in the general dance.

Thomas Merton

Dabar: five letters, one Hebrew word, written by the Fire of a Secret Hand in myriad ways.[1] Each letter of *dabar* is a radiant body that offers to cast away the last vestiges of our "awful solemnity," and carry us into a festival of deeper life. Each sacred syllable, each crownlet of each *dabar* is a passage-way to a greener land: the Narnia within Narnia Charles Lindbergh discovered on the eighteenth hour of his historical flight, when he sensed himself as "an awareness spreading through space, over the earth and into the heavens, unhampered by time or substance. . . ."[2]

Meaning literally "word," *dabar* is an Abyss of Mercy, which defies translation.

For the Hebrew, the *word* and the one who speaks it are the same—which is why the Old Testament describes Solomon's life by the phrase: "the words of Solomon."

Dabar and the Secret One are the same: the *word* is the expression of his thought, his passion of silent devotion.

One Rebbe understood this identity between the word and the speaker so clearly that he would go into ecstasy whenever the Maggid prefaced his public reading of scripture by saying: "And God spoke." The Rebbe had to be escorted out of the room into the hall, where he would call out to anyone who cared to listen: "God speaks! Do you understand, my brothers, can you believe such a thing could happen: God *speaks!*"

> As the Baal Shem lay upon the bottom of the Vessel, a lone and silent Thing, a Heavenly Voice, rose quite gently and began to speak within him, first simply, and as at home, but always swelling, and becoming mightier, until at last the Voice swallowed the howling of the ocean that was lost as a whisper within her call. And the Master drank the sound of the Voice of God. . . .[3]

* * *

So *dabar* is more than "word," more than sound or meaning. *Dabar* is event, dynamic happening—like the *vac* of the ancient Vedas: "the word," the firstborn of the Absolute. Grammatically feminine, this "daughter" expresses deep surrender to the Source from which she springs: "All this, in the beginning, was only the Lord of the universe. His Word was with Him. This word was his second. He contemplated. He said, 'I will deliver this Word so that she will produce and bring into being all this world.' "[4]

So the "daughter" in this Vedic text becomes a "mother." Springing from the womb of the Absolute, she becomes *dabar:* the creative energy of the Secret One.

When the Book of Genesis recalls the first event of creation on *yom ehad,* it is in terms of *dabar,* the mother: "God speaks, saying: Let there be light." "Through *dabar* the heavens were made," the psalmist sings, "and by *dabar* the heavens continue to breathe." The joy of fire and hail, he chants, is to "fulfill" *dabar,* who gathers the waters of every sea as in a flask, and in her kindness spreads out snow like wool, and scatters frost like ashes.

Dabar is *hitlahavut,* the ecstasy of a woman who nourishes and sustains her offspring. She is intelligent: all she does is for the purpose of transforming the pilgrim into the likeness of God—the way she did in the desert father Anastasius' life.

One day Anastasius discovered that his Bible was missing. When the robber—a man who had visited the abba—went to sell the book, the buyer said: "Leave it with me, so that I can be sure it's worth the sixteen pence you're asking for it."

The buyer took the Bible to Abba Anastasius.

"Do you think this is worth sixteen pence?"

"Yes," the old man said.

When the buyer told the robber about his meeting with Anastasius, the man's eyes widened.

"That's all he said? Nothing more? You're sure?"

"No, nothing else. Why? Have you changed your mind?"

"Yes," the robber said, snatching the Bible out of the buyer's hands. "I've changed my mind."

The robber hurried through the streets, into the wilderness —all the while led by a secret messenger, the holy body of *dabar.*

Once inside Abba Anastasius' dwelling, the robber hurled himself at the old man's feet.

"Forgive me," he said, tears streaming down his face, "I didn't know what I was doing. Take the Bible back, please. I'll never sleep unless you do. . . ."

"Peace be with you, my son. Come, rise to your feet. Of course I forgive you. As for the Bible, I want you to have it as a gift. That you may continue to know the tears of Christ and the mercy of his Abba, and the power of his *dabar* in your heart all the days of your life."

* * *

The psalmist sings of a Friend who "sends forth" his word —a messenger who "runs quickly."

Dabar is a messenger who appears in myriad disguises—but always with the same message, the same questions: "Are you uplifting the world with your words? And giving birth to angels by your deeds?"

To which he adds a third question: "Are you aware that every person and every thing and every event is a Secret Love?"

> . . . It is the love of God that sends the winter days when I am cold and sick, and the hot summer when I labor and my clothes are full of sweat: but it is God Who breathes on me with light winds off the river and in the breezes out of the wood. His love spreads the shade of the syca-more over my head and sends the water-boy along the edge of the wheat field with a bucket from the spring, while the laborers are resting and the mules stand under the tree.[5]

The Holy One leaves it up to each messenger to make up her own disguise, and to sing her own song, in her own way.

The Holy Rebbe's sole concern is that, when heard, *dabar* might awaken a spark of paradise in the heart of the pilgrim.

And an angel be born into the world.

On Becoming
the Song of Songs

The Maggid [of Mezritch] once said to his disciples:
"I shall teach you the best way to say Torah. You must
cease to be aware of yourselves. You must be nothing but
an ear which hears what the universe of the word is
constantly saying within you. The moment you start
hearing what you yourself are saying, you must stop."
Martin Buber

Sacred Scripture is one of the many "events" of *dabar*. It is
the "Word of God" in a very special way.

It is said that the Baal Shem Tov was deeply taken with The
Song of Songs—the great canticle of silent devotion we find in
the Old Testament. With good reason: the Song of Songs
expresses the kernel of every scriptural word: the unconditional
giving of the Secret One, and his power to transform the
listener into the likeness of God.

Let me tell you what happened "once upon a time," when
the night was in midcourse and the poplar forest asleep, and
the power of *dabar* began to flow into the ears of the Maggid
of Mezritch.

It happened on a Friday. Rabbi Aaron had eaten supper in
the Maggid's house. It was late, so the rabbi went back to his

inn and began to pray the Song of Songs—in a whisper, so as not to disturb anyone.

A bit later, he heard a knock at the door. It was the servant of the Maggid, looking embarrassed, like a boy who has rung the wrong doorbell.

"It's the Song of Songs," he said softly.

"What did you say?"

"The Maggid cannot sleep . . . because the Song of Songs is roaring through his room. . . ."

* * *

Because the Secret One is all-knowing, he can see the entire body of mankind in one glance. So when he speaks his *dabar* to Abraham or Habacuc or Peter, he is also speaking in a deeply personal way to each unique cell of that universal body. *Dabar* arrives with the precise word I need at a given stage of my journey. The responsorial psalm of today's Mass brings out this personal concern of *dabar:* "If you could listen to the word I have for you, I would feed you with the finest wheat, and fill your heart with honey from the rock. . . ."

But I have to do more than "read" *dabar.* I'm called to listen to its song in faith, as to someone I love:

> As today writing after three days of rain
> Hearing the wren sing and the falling cease
> And bowing not knowing to what.[1]

Silent, I listen. The scriptural text open, I hear a word, a phrase, a sentence. The voice of the Secret One speaks, then vanishes into the furthest limits of "this clay jug." And I bow down, not knowing to what.

The wren sings, its sound disappears, and I bow down in the silence, again and again. I bow down inside the Love of the Friend through whose hands "the planets in all the galaxies/ pass . . . like beads."[2] My heart whispers *"namasté,"* again and again.

*   *   *

It happened that Abba Anthony wanted to test some of the other desert fathers who came to visit him. He suggested a text from the Scriptures and asked each of them to explain its meaning.

Everyone expounded—except for one: Abba Joseph, who kept silent.

"And you," Anthony said, "what do you have to say?"

"Nothing," Joseph said. "I have nothing to say. I don't know."

Anthony looked steadily at the other desert fathers and said: "See, of all of you Abba Joseph is the only one who knows the way, because he does not know."

Dabar engages the whole person, beginning at the level of "not knowing": the way that lies beyond the fiftieth gate of knowledge in a loving silence beyond concepts or images. And from there it sweeps back through all the other gates: feelings, imagination, senses: "By the sweetness of its sound it soothes your affections, by its abounding wealth of meaning it nourishes and strengthens your mind, by the depth of its mystery it bewilders the intellect."

St. Bernard wrote these words in the twelfth century. In those days, the traditional way of penetrating to the heart of *dabar* was through *lectio divina:* literally, "divine reading." *Lectio* was the way Bernard listened to the secret sound of *dabar:* through loving-knowledge, wisdom-knowledge.

When we listen to dabar in this way and flow with the fragrance of its wisdom, we become *dabar*—so that gradually every scriptural word becomes our *dabar,* and the Song of Songs our song. Then every crownlet of every sacred letter begins to express our depth, flowing from the Heart of a Greater Depth—a Giant disguised as a messenger running with rapid, singing strides.

We become the Speaker in His Abyss of Mercy, and his secret sound, and the listener too.

By becoming *dabar,* we flow deeper into the center of a feast in the wilderness—where every living thing is a friend, spiraling out in concentric circles from the Depth of the Great Round Dance.

How good it is to be *dabar,* the Secret One inside us, through whose hands the planets in all the galaxies pass like beads!

How good to be the Song of Songs, roaring through canyons and pine mountains, and the ears of the Maggid of Mezritch!

Where Is the *Duende*?

The *duende* . . . Where is the *duende*? Through the empty
arch comes a wind . . . a wind that [announces] the
constant baptism of newly created things.
　　　　　　　　　　　　Federico Garcia Lorca

On days when I sing with *duende,* no one can touch me.
　　　　　　　　　　　　El Lebrijano

Andalusia. Wherever you go, you hear the same word: in the
streets of Cádiz, where lovers walk hand in hand, in the out-
skirts of tiny villages where children learn *canto hondo,* in the
deep night of Granada where gypsies gather to fling their
ballads into the waters of the Mediterranean.

Duende.

Lorca tells this story: The Andalusian singer Pastora Pavón
is entertaining in a little tavern in Cádiz. Her "voice of shadow, of beaten tin"[1] drives the audience into a heavy cloud. She
finishes her song: nothing. No applause. Someone murmurs:
"Viva Paris!" Meaning: "Here skill means nothing!"

Suddenly Pastora Pavón leaps to her feet, and begins to sing
again: "And how she sang! Her voice was no longer playing
. . . it opened like a ten-fingered hand, . . ." Lorca recalls, "pure
music with a body so lean it could stay in the air."[2]

The Andalusians roared their approval: Pastora Pavón had sung with *duende!*

* * *

Sometimes—rarely—you hear about *duende* outside of Spain. In Germany, Goethe described it once—while talking about Paganini—as a force which everyone feels, but philosophers cannot define.

"The *duende* is not in the throat," an old maestro of the guitar told Lorca. "The *duende* climbs up inside you, from the soles of the feet."[3]

"From the soles of the feet": as from roots to branches.

To sense *duende* you have to pass through the gate King David exalted in Psalm 118: the gate which belongs to the Secret One, the passage to thanksgiving, and the rock the builders cast away. To meet *duende* you have to be willing to pass beyond the fiftieth gate.

> "We're coming near," said the driver. Where were we? At the foot of the mountain, thank God . . . We were in the valley. Sighet: 40 kilometers. Sighet: 30 kilometers. A multitude of huts formed a hedge along the road. Villages sprang up before our headlights and were immediately swallowed again by the night. Far away, there were a few blinking lights. Sighet: 20 kilometers. The car, an old Volga, picked up speed. Sighet: 15 kilometers. "We're coming near," the driver repeated in a heavy voice. His words sounded like a threat. He was taking me to a rendezvous. With whom? With death? With myself? Sighet: 10 kilometers . . .[4]

Duende.

An untranslatable word, one that can only be experienced in the marrow. *Duende* means, roughly, "Death is with me on my journey as a fellow pilgrim—every step of the way."

Outside of Spain, Lorca says, when someone passes away, they shut the curtains; in Spain they open them: "And just as

Germany has, with few exceptions, muse, and Italy shall always have angel, so in all ages Spain is moved by the *duende,* for it is a country of ancient music and dance where the *duende* squeezes the lemons of dawn—a country of death. A country open to death."5

Not so elsewhere. In most countries, to speak of death is a taboo, a social blunder. In the United States, at a seminar on death and dying, a twenty-eight-year-old nurse and mother of four, who was in the last stages of cancer, asked the audience, "How would you feel if you came into a hospital room to visit a twenty-eight-year-old mother dying of cancer?"6 The answers: angry, confused, full of horror, full of pity, sad, frustrated. Then the nurse put another question to the group: "Suppose *you* were the twenty-eight-year-old mother dying of cancer—how would you feel if everyone who walked into the room came in with those feelings?"

Suddenly the group understood how much they had surrounded the patient with their own reactions to death—and ignored *her* and how things *were.* They saw how much they had overlooked the twenty-eight-year-old mother of four—a woman who needed, and deserved, to be understood.

Meeting *duende* does not mean that we know when—or how—we will die. The nurse did not have to be terminally ill to know the power of *duende.*

To live with *duende* means that—following an important turning point—we begin to flow more in context—more as a continuum of experience that stretches from birth until after death.

This is what makes *duende* and the virtue of hope such friends. They resemble two delicate flowers touching each other lightly. Like *duende,* hope lives in the present moment— and beyond it, in *azaliat,* eternal time.

The research of Dr. Raymond Moody has done much to verify this wider vision of life. His investigation of hundreds of people pronounced clinically dead and later revived has weakened some of the impact of the taboo on death. Besides the rendezvous with the Being of Light, these people report feeling intense love, peace, and joy. They tell of being with others, and visiting celestial realms: cities of light whose description coincides with images we find in Scripture. Dr. Moody's findings affirm *duende* as a passageway of hope.

And yet, despite the extensive research by Dr. Moody, it remains true that the taboo on death is still shaping the attitudes of many people—which should not surprise us, if we remember what Christ has Abraham saying in St. Luke's Gospel: "If they can't hear what Moses and the prophets are saying, neither will they be convinced if someone rises from the dead."

"And the *duende,* where is the *duende?*"

Ask Abraham—he'll tell you. He's finished the journey.

"Right behind you, my friend. The *duende* is behind you with his questions, always the same questions: 'Are you uplifting the world with your words. . . . ?' "

"The *duende,* where is the *duende?*"

Through the empty arch the sound of a gentle wind, moving slowly past an open checkpoint. . . .

* * *

We come out of the mother naked. And old. With wrinkled skin, and sightless eyes. But how we return to the Mother of Silence and Light, the Mother of Love—is another question.

Our pilgrimage is a return to childhood in the Gospel sense: a recovery of our "original features," in the image of the Secret One.

Last year I read *The Unblinding,* a book of poems by Laurence Lieberman. To become a child is to "unblind": to see with the eyes of silence, love and light, in the likeness of God.

And the *duende?*

Death is the flow from silence and love to deeper silence and greater love. *Duende* is the light that takes us beyond an open checkpoint, to a continuation of the "unblinding" we have begun in this body as an old child, with these senses and this mind.

*   *   *

As the Baal Shem Tov lay dying, he tried to console his disciples.

"My sons," he whispered with infinite tenderness, "don't weep. Can't you see that I have to go through one door if I am to pass through the next?"

Then he closed his eyes, and was gone.

Later on, his disciples confirmed the rumor: at the moment of his death they had seen a bright blue flame rise up from the bed of the Baal Shem Tov, and ascend into the silence of the heavens.

> To live is to rush ahead eating up your own death,
> like an endgate, open, hurrying into night.[7]

Sometimes it takes more than a lifetime to come to the age of a child.

A Full Circle of Light

> You have noticed that everything an Indian does is in a
> circle, and that is because the Power of the World always
> works in circles, and everything tries to be round. In the
> old days when we were a strong and happy people, all
> our power came to us from the sacred hoop of the nation
> . . . Everything the Power of the World does is done in
> a circle . . . The wind, in its greatest power, whirls. Birds
> make their nests in circles . . . Our teepees were round
> like the nests of birds, and these were always set in a
> circle . . . But the Wasichus have put us in these square
> boxes. . . .
>
> *Black Elk*

The Native American sees life as a flow through various
worlds of light into a full circle of light: the mystery of oneness.

The Indian learns at an early age to "go in circles," to take
part in the round dances of his tribal elders. For the Native,
the dance is a way to "grow up," to go beyond the "little ego,"
and ultimately to pass beyond the edge of the great circle of
light. The Native Wovoka warned: "All Indians must dance,
everywhere, keep on dancing. Pretty soon in next spring Great
Spirit come . . . Indians who don't dance . . . will grow little,
just about a foot high, and stay that way. . . ."[1]

Usually the Indian dances alone: in the sense that the hermit sings alone in the wilderness. When the Indian carries bells and feathers and shells and bracelets in his dance, he is carrying the world as well. When he follows the rhythm of the drumbeat, so is the Great Spirit inside him. Like the hermit in the wilderness, the Indian is a great assembly.

The Native's dance symbolizes the Friend who whirls in the center of the Great Round Dance—a Full Body that knows distinctions on the surface and no duality at the roots: no Greek, no Jew, no male, no female, no sane, no insane. No "one" opposed to other "ones." Only relationship grounded in oneness, moving to a full circle of light: the new creation.

*   *   *

The pilgrim who travels through the wilderness is part of a collective journey: the return of the cosmos to its Destiny in the Heart of the Great Round Dance.

> Those apples grow from the Gift, and they sink back
> into the Gift.
> It must be that they are coming from the garden to the
> garden.[2]

This return is a cosmic celebration of *duende:* the rushing ahead of each particle of creation into deeper levels of "unblinding." It is the collective song of *Ani ledodi,* in which the universe moves as one Body across the surface of the ages, to its fulfillment in the *eschaton:* history's culmination in the Silence of a Secret Destiny, and a Love which never ceases.

> Die now, die now, in this Love die; when you have
> died in this Love, you will all receive new life. . . .

> Die now, die now, and come forth from this cloud;
> when you come forth from this cloud, you will all be
> radiant full moons . . .[3]

* * *

The Book of Genesis recalls the first stirring of this convergence on the eschaton. The journey begins on *yom ehad.* Life evolves from the inorganic to the organic, moves from the mineral kingdom through the vegetable and animal kingdoms, and expands to include the first man and woman.

This convergence has continued to the present day. Each of us is part of this trackless mass of energy going home, rushing through every pocket of the universe with the speed of *duende:* through locked doors and buried gardens and old children— resurrecting, restoring, sustaining . . . all the time adding new cells to the Collective Body of the Secret One.

* * *

The Native American principle of the *ho-ko-ka*[4] is simple: everything has to come full circle. One begins with effort, but graduates into the ease of a river giving itself back to its source.

The pilgrim is part of a vast flow into the fullness of Light: a tiny leaf on an immense tree, whose life is a progressive "unblinding": a journey from garden to garden.

Today is the Fourth Sunday of Lent. We're close to the Feast that celebrates the resurrection of the Universal Body of Christ into the fullness of the eschaton: a process already finished, yet hidden from our eyes.

The theme of the Preface of the Great Eucharistic Prayer today is the man who "unblinds" in the Gospel of St. John, the one who tells his neighbors: "A Rabbi put mud on my eyes, and when I washed it off, I could see!"

The Preface responds to this by chanting, "Earth is joining hands with heaven to sing the new song of creation": the collective unblinding of the cosmos into the fullness of *Ani ledodi.*

The liturgy underlines the spaciousness of this song of unblinding. The texts of the Mass include everyone: angels, saints, pilgrims of every kind, as well as bread and wine, to show that even matter is sweeping to its Destiny in the Heart of a Secret Friend.

The Eucharistic Prayer culminates in a doxology: "Through, with, and in Christ—in the unity of the Holy Spirit —all glory and honor is yours, Almighty Father, forever and ever."

The circle is closed, the return to the eschaton completed: *ho-ko-ka.*

In Christ the "honor and glory," the radiance of the cosmos, is offered as gift to the Gift. But at the same time the doxology describes this surrender of the universe back to the Secret One as paradox: relationship within nonduality.

Christ offers the cosmos *to* his Abba: but in the oneness, the unity of the Holy Spirit.

The liturgical texts of the Feast of Christ the King bring out this collective paradox. In the first reading, the Secret One promises his people "rest": a biblical symbol of the silence of nonduality, oneness. Then the Gospel depicts the Secret One as Lover, the Being of Light who identifies with the poor at the Last Judgment: "I was hungry and you gave me bread, thirsty and you gave me water to drink. . . ." But in between these two images we find a letter by St. Paul that says that at the end of time Christ will hand over the Kingdom to his Father.

> Far out at the edge of the heron's wing,
> where the air is disturbed by the last feather,
> there is the Kingdom. . . .[5]

This Kingdom is the flowering of the cosmos, a tree having grown through *duende* into a paradox of concurrent oneness (rest) and relationship (love). At the end, Christ will place the gift of this collective paradox—his Full Body—into the luminous hands of the Gift of Abba—a Body so full that, as Paul senses in his letter, the Secret One will be "all in all."

This "all in all" is Black Elk finally freed from his square house, ecstatic, dancing a Great Round Dance at the furthest edge of the Heron's wing. It is the apex of *ho-ko-ka:* the fulfillment of the shared grace of *duende,* the celebration of *Ani ledodi* in a Full Circle of Light.

The Last Dance

At last the three companions turned away, and never again looking back they rode slowly homewards; and they spoke no word to one another until they came back to the Shire, but each had great comfort in his friends on the long grey road.

At last they rode over the downs and took the East Road, and then Merry and Pippin rode on to Buckland; and already they were singing again as they went. But Sam turned to Bywater, and so came back up the Hill, as day was ending once more. And he went on, and there was yellow light, and fire within; and the evening meal was ready, and he was expected. And Rose drew him in, and set him in his chair, and put little Elanor upon his lap.

He drew a deep breath. "Well, I'm back," he said.

The End

J. R. R. Tolkien

Monastic life has been called "the angelic life." There is deep truth in this description, one reason being that the monk of "this clay jug"—the pilgrim—is *malakh:* the Hebrew word for "angel," which also means "messenger."

Each pilgrim is connected to every other cell of the cosmic body of the universe. He (or she) is a messenger who, by being sensitive to the Secret One, arrives with the precise *dabar* needed at a given moment. So this morning, when I heard that a pilgrim had appeared at the monastery gate, I wondered why this man had been sent here, and to whom, and with what message, what hope, what secret.

"Who is he?"

Brother Nathanael shrugged.

"A dancer from New York, I think. A young man in blue jeans, with a beard and long black hair. He's very poor—because he chooses to be."

After chanting None, about sixty monks gather in the chapter room. Fascinated, they watch the man do one dance after another across the pebbled floor.

"My friends, this will be the last dance."

The young man announces that he will end his visit with a tribute to Father Isaac, whom he loves and admires, whose books he has read, whom he wishes he could have met.

But Isaac is away, in Asia, at a monastic conference.

Now the dancer, looking very serious, moves slowly to the table near the abbot's chair.

Meticulously, and with reverence, he pulls on a white cowl: a long flowing garment with wide sleeves reaching down to the ankles, the centuries-old garment of the Cistercian monk.

The dancer moves slowly to the table by the prior's chair, and switches on a tape recorder: a gypsy melody, haunting and deep, the ancient music of Andalusia.

Now the young man is in the center of the room.

He begins to dance round and round the chapter room like a burning wheel: a bucket of fire spinning round, carrying monks and benches and doors and windows in its heart.

Suddenly, without warning, like a tide turning, the dancer sweeps around in the direction of the west door. And flows out of the room, into the long cloister with its empty corridors, over a century old. A thousand centuries of silence old.

Flowing like a sea . . . enticed, charmed, not knowing why. Not knowing how . . . or when, or where. . . .

Echoes.

Listen.

Do you hear them?

Faint, short echoes, fading away . . . softer, quieter.

Softer, fainter, fainter. . . .

Silence.

In the chapter room, nobody moves. Nobody.

Click.

The tape recorder snaps off, sending a sharp echo springing off the stone walls.

Still nobody moves. The silence is dense, tearing the air.

At last one of the monks turns slowly to his neighbor, leans over and whispers something in his ear.

"That means Isaac isn't coming back."

* * *

The monk was right.

Two weeks later, Isaac was dead—by a freak accident in his hotel room in Asia. Curiously, on the anniversary of his entrance into the monastery.

I opened the chapter room door leading into the rock garden, and walked over to the almond tree.

The fresh air felt good.

Suddenly, I heard a voice behind me.

"*Namasté.*"

I whirled around.

It was *him*—it was the Rebbe with his questions, the Great Blue Heron with bright wings long as Holland!

With a slow, graceful gesture the Rebbe motioned to me to come, and follow him.

"Where?" I asked.

He said nothing.

But after a long, long moment he looked into my eyes and spoke.

"Home," he said. "It's time to go home."

I would like to tell you that I dropped everything right there, and ran behind him.

But the truth is that I hesitated.

I paused beneath the almond tree, looking for several long seconds across the highway at the hills I loved, and felt the snowflakes fall gently across my face.

Then I turned back to the Rebbe.

"Now?" I asked, quietly.

"Yes," he said. "Now."

I turned my back on the high monastery wall, and the steeple arching into the sky, and followed him home.

Notes

The Hasidic and Desert Father stories you find in these notes often do not correspond exactly to the historical accounts in traditional sources. This is because the versions in these pages are interpretations intended by the author to illustrate or emphasize some "ground tone." For example, the original Hasidic story of the fiftieth gate says nothing about the "tender hand of faith" expecting someone "like a woman awaiting her beloved after a long voyage at sea." Nor does the original Desert Father story mention *dabar* leading the robber to Abba Anastasius, and the old man's words of encouragement as recorded in these notes. For the most part, however, the versions are faithful in their essential components to the original sources, which are as follows:

Elie Wiesel, *Souls on Fire* (New York: Vintage Books, 1972).

Elie Wiesel, *Four Hasidic Masters and Their Struggle Against Melancholy* (Notre Dame: University of Notre Dame Press, 1978).

Martin Buber, *Tales of the Hasidim: Early Masters* (New York: Schocken Books, 1947).

In Praise of the Baal Shem Tov: The Earliest Collection of Legends about the Founder of Hasidim, translated and edited by Dan Ben-Amos and Jerome R. Mintz (Bloomington: Indiana University Press, 1970).

The Wisdom of the Desert: Sayings from the Desert Fathers of the Fourth Century, translated by Thomas Merton (New York: New Directions, 1970).

Sayings of the Desert Fathers, translated by Benedicta Ward (Kalamazoo: Cistercian Publications, 1975).

Most of the scriptural quotations are versions by the author. All poetry selections are fragments of a complete work, except for the opening quotation of Chapter Five.

The quotations that appear in each chapter are intended by the author to illustrate a given point. These excerpts have been drawn from their original context and adapted by the author to a new set of circumstances. They do not always reflect the original meaning intended by a quoted author.

Dedication
A Film Trilogy (New York: The Orion Press, 1967), p. 26.

Prologue
Opening quotation: Robert Bly, *Sleepers Joining Hands* (New York: Harper and Row, 1973), p. 8.
[1] *The Kabir Book: Forty-four of the Ecstatic Poems of Kabir,* Versions by Robert Bly (Boston: Beacon Press, 1977), p 7.
[2] Ram Dass, *Grist for the Mill* (Santa Cruz: Unity Press, 1977), p. 15.
[3] Galway Kinnell, *The Avenue Bearing the Initial of Christ into the New World: Poems 1946–1964* (Boston: Houghton Mifflin Company, 1974), p. 132.
[4] Robert Bly, *The Morning Glory* (New York: Harper and Row, 1975), p. 45.
[5] Robert Bly, *The Morning Glory,* p. 45.

Chapter One
Opening quotation: Charles Simic, *Dismantling the Silence* (New York: George Braziller, Inc., 1971), p. 16.

Chapter Two
In the issue of *Quest/79,* pp. 98–100, "Independent Icelander," Janet Hobhouse notes that the paintings of Louisa Matthiasdottir describe a "brightly painted fisherman's cottage, the sweeps of the horizons (of Iceland), treeless and flat, yet oddly domestic." She recalls the "particular coolness of Icelandic light, shapes of the land reaches in the fjords, the blue of the water that surrounds the land everywhere, the purple and rust of the Icelandic rock."

Chapter Three
Opening Quotation: Charles Simic, *Dismantling the Silence,* p. 45.
[1] Elie Wiesel, *Legends of Our Time* (New York: Avon Books, 1968), p. 124.
[2] *The Kabir Book,* p. 57.
[3] Jalal al-Din Rumi. Version of a poem by Rumi by Robert Bly, in *Talking All Morning* (Ann Arbor: The University of Michigan Press, 1980), p. 236.

Chapter Four
Opening Quotation: Elie Wiesel, *Legends of Our Time,* p 31.
[1] Gerard Manley Hopkins, *The Poems of Gerard Manley Hopkins* (London: Oxford University Press, 1967), p. 66.
[2] *Ibid.*
[3] This term is according to Robert Bly's translation in *The Kabir Book.*

4 Robert Bly, *The Kabir Book,* p. 59.

5 James Wright, *The Branch Will Not Break* (Middletown: Wesleyan University Press, 1962), p. 35.

6 Pima, "Foot Race Song," translated by Frank Russell, appearing in *News of the Universe: Poems of Twofold Consciousness,* chosen and introduced by Robert Bly (San Francisco: Sierra Club Books, 1980), p. 262.

7 *Ibid.*

Chapter Five

Opening quotation: *The Kabir Book,* p. 6.

1 Robert Bly, *Lorca and Jiménez: Selected Poems,* chosen and translated by Robert Bly (Boston: Beacon Press, 1973), pp. 101–102.

2 Juan Ramon Jiménez, translated by Robert Bly, in *Lorca and Jiménez,* p. 79.

3 Nikos Kazantzakis, *The Odyssey: A Modern Sequel* (New York: Simon and Schuster, 1969), p. 478.

4 Federico Garcia Lorca, *Deep Song and Other Prose,* edited and translated by Christopher Maurer (New York: New Directions, 1980), p. 50. The author applies the term *flamenco woman* in a context different from that intended by Federico Lorca.

5 Charles Simic, *Dismantling the Silence,* p. 53.

Chapter Six

Opening Quotation: Bede Griffiths, *Return to the Center* (Springfield, Ill.: Templegate, 1976), pp. 61 and 59. The author has combined excerpts from these two pages into one paragraph.

1 Elie Wiesel translates the verse as "I belong to my beloved as my beloved belongs to me." See *Four Hasidic Masters and their struggle against Melancholy,* p. 32.

2 The Prophecy of Hosea (2:14–15), from *The Holy Bible: A Translation From the Latin Vulgate in the Light of the Hebrew and Greek Originals* (New York: Sheed and Ward, Inc., 1950), p. 810.

Chapter Seven

Opening Quotation: C. S. Lewis, *The Last Battle* (New York: Macmillan, 1970), pp. 170–171.

1 Raimundo Panikkar, *The Trinity and the Religious Experience of Man* (New York: Orbis Books, 1973), p. 45.

2 Hermann Hesse, translation by Robert Bly, in *News of the Universe,* p. 86.

Chapter Eight

Opening Quotation: Nikos Kazantzakis, *The Last Temptation of Christ* (New York: Simon and Schuster, 1966), p. 63.

[1] Rabindranath Tagore, *Gitanjali* (New York: Macmillan, 1971), p. 93.

[2] Meister Eckhart. From *Meister Eckhart,* ed. Franz Pfeiffer, trans. C. de B. Evans (London: John M. Watkins, 1947), p. 59. I have quoted John S. Dunne's version of this translation. See: John S. Dunne, *The Reasons of the Heart* (New York: Macmillan, 1978), p. 48.

[3] Juan Ramón Jiménez, translated by Robert Bly, in *Lorca and Jiménez,* p. 23.

[4] Proverbs 6:27.

[5] Robert Bly, *This Body Is Made of Camphor and Gopherwood* (New York: Harper and Row, 1971), p. 59.

[6] Martin Buber, *The Legend of the Baal-Shem* (New York: Schocken Books, 1969), p. 17.

[7] Elie Wiesel, *A Jew Today* (New York: Random House, 1978), pp. 182–183.

Chapter Nine

Opening Quotation: Nikos Kazantzakis, *The Last Temptation of Christ,* p. 240.

[1] Nikos Kazantzakis, *Report to Greco* (New York: Simon and Schuster, 1965), p. 55.

[2] J.R.R. Tolkien, *The Return of the King* (New York: Ballantine Books, 1965), p. 384.

[3] See Elie Wiesel, *Souls on Fire,* p. 31.

Chapter Ten

Opening Quotation: Carlos Castaneda, *Journey to Ixtlan: The Lessons of Don Juan* (New York: Simon and Schuster, 1972), p. 107.

[1] Rumi, in *Talking All Morning,* p. 236.

[2] Caryll Houselander, *The Reed of God* (New York: Arena Lettres, 1978), p. 1.

[3] Franz Kafka, *The Basic Kafka* (New York: Pocket Books, 1979), pp. 185–186.

Chapter Eleven

Opening Quotation: Nikos Kazantzakis, *Report to Greco,* p. 234.

[1] Quoted in Federico Lorca, *Deep Song and Other Prose,* p. 67.

[2] Federico Lorca, *Deep Song and Other Prose,* p. 30.

[3] *Ibid.,* p. 32.

[4] *Ibid.,* p. 40.

[5] Thomas Merton, *New Seeds of Contemplation* (New York: New Directions, 1961), p. 29.

[6] *Ibid.,* p. 29.

[7] Thomas Merton, *The Seven Storey Mountain* (Garden City: Image Books, 1970), pp. 510–512.

8 A fragment of an unpublished Syriac hymn by St. Ephraim, fifth century. Quoted in *Teach Us to Pray,* by André Louf (New York: Paulist Press, 1974), p. 97.

Chapter Twelve
Opening Quotation: Thomas Merton, *The Sign of Jonas* (Garden City: Image Books, 1953), pp. 351–52.
1 Ram Dass, From "On Lay Monasticism," in *Journal of Transpersonal Psychology,* 1977, Vol. 9, No. 2., p. 135. The Brother in this passage is not Jonas.
2 Jalal al-Din Rumi, *Mystical Poems of Rumi,* translated from the Persian by A. J. Arberry (Chicago: The University of Chicago Press, 1968), p. 82.

Chapter Thirteen
Opening Quotation: Thomas Merton, *The Sign of Jonas,* pp. 339, 344–345.
1 Joshu Sasaki Roshi, *Zen The Root of Being,* Cross Currents, Vol. XXIV, Number 2–3, Summer-Fall, 1974, p. 204. See also: p. 393, description by Brother David Steindl-Rast of the conclusion of the symposium. The author has borrowed a term Brother David uses—"bow of gratitude"—in the acknowledgment page.
2 W. S. Merwin, *The Moving Target* (New York: Atheneum, 1963), pp. 80–81.
3 Elie Wiesel, *The Gates of the Forest* (New York: Avon Books, 1966), pp. 192, 198.
4 Rumi, *Mystical Poems of Rumi,* p. 86.
5 Robert Bly, *The Morning Glory,* p. 68.
6 C.S. Lewis, *Perelandra* (New York: Macmillan, 1947), pp. 229–235.
7 Rumi, *Mystical Poems of Rumi,* p. 92.

Chapter Fourteen
Opening Quotation: Thomas Merton, *New Seeds of Contemplation,* p. 297.
1 See: Lawrence Kushner, *Honey From the Rock* (New York: Harper and Row, 1977), p. 12.
For more on *dabar,* see: *Theological Dictionary of the Old Testament,* Vol. III, ed. by Johannes Botterweck and Helmer Ringgren (Grand Rapids: William B. Eerdmans Publishing Company, 1978), pp. 84–125. See also: *Dictionary of Biblical Theology,* edited under the direction of Xavier Leon-Dufour (New York: Seabury Press, 1962), pp. 868–872.
2 Charles Lindbergh relates this experience in *The Spirit of St. Louis* (New York: Scribner, 1953).
3 Meyer Levin, *Classic Hassidic Tales* (New York: Penguin Books, 1932, 1975), p. 161.

4 From the Vedas, quoted in "The Silence of the Word: Nondualistic
Polarities," by Raimundo Panikkar. *Cross Currents.*, p. 156. See also: Panikkar, *The Vedic Experience* (Berkeley: University of California Press, 1977),
p. 89. Raimundo Panikkar.
5 Thomas Merton, *New Seeds of Contemplation,* pp. 16–17.

Chapter Fifteen
Opening Quotation: Martin Buber, *Tales of the Hasidim: Early Masters,*
p. 107.
1 W. S. Merwin, *The Lice* (New York: Atheneum, 1979), p. 58.
2 *The Kabir Book,* p. 29.

Chapter Sixteen
Opening Quotation: Federico Lorca, *Deep Song and Other Prose,* pp. 53,
43.
1 *Ibid.,* p. 45.
2 *Ibid.,* p. 46. Lorca says: "La Niña de los Peines had to tear her voice
because she knew she had an exquisite audience, one which demanded not
forms but the marrow of forms, pure music with a body so lean it could stay
in the air."
3 *Ibid.,* p. 43.
4 Elie Wiesel, *Legends of Our Time,* p. 148.
5 Federico Lorca, *Deep Song and Other Prose,* p. 47.
6 Ram Dass, *Grist for the Mill,* p. 128. For more on Dr. Moody's research
on death, see his books *Life After Life* (New York: Bantam Books, 1977)
and *Reflections on Life After Life* (New York: Bantam Books, 1978).
7 Robert Bly, *This Tree Will Be Here for a Thousand Years* (New York:
Harper and Row, 1979), p. 25.

Chapter Seventeen
Opening Quotation: John G. Neihardt, *Black Elk Speaks: Being the Life
Story of a Holy Man of the Oglala Sioux* (New York: Pocket Books, 1972),
pp. 164–66.
1 Quoted in *Dance Into Life: The Native American Way,* by José Hobday,
Cross Currents, p. 292. This article provides background material for the
first page of this chapter.
2 Rumi, in *Talking All Morning,* p. 236.
3 Rumi, *Mystical Poems of Rumi,* p. 70.
4 *Cross Currents,* p. 344. From remarks by Sr. José Hobday.
5 Robert Bly, *Sleepers Joining Hands,* p. 8.

Chapter Eighteen
Opening Quotation: J. R. R. Tolkien, *The Return of the King,* pp. 384–
385.

Glossary

Ah - "a" as in the "o" in "not."
Ay - "a" as in "stay."
Eh - "e" as in "let."
Gh - "g" as in "get."
Oh - "o" as in "soar."

ABBA: Áh-bah: an Aramaic term Christ uses to designate "The Father."
   Abba also means "desert father."
ANI LEDODI: Áh-nee leh-doh-dée: See Chapter 6.
BAAL SHEM TOV: Bahl Shehm Tóhv: founder of the Hasidic movement in the eighteenth century.
CANTAOR: cahn-tah-óhr: singer.
CANTO HONDO: cáhntoh hóndoh: deep song.
DABAR: dah-báhr: word.
DUENDE: doo-éhn-deh: See Chapter 14.
EBOLI: Éh-boh-lee: part of the title of an Italian film.
HASID: Hah-séed: one who loves.
HESED: héh-sehd: loving-kindness.
HITLAHAVUT: hiht-lah-havoót: the ardor of ecstasy.
MAGGID: mah-ghéed: A Jewish preacher.
MONOS: móh-nohs: one.
MOSHE: Móh-sheh: Moses.
NAMASTÉ: Nah-mah-stáy: See Prologue.
RUAH: Roó-ah: spirit, breath, wind.
RUMI: Roó-mee: a Turkish poet.
YOM EHAD: yohm ehúd: day one.